W9-AHN-361

Katie Brown's
Outdoor Entertaining

Katie Brown's
Outdoor Entertaining
Taking the Party Outside

.Photography by Paul Whicheloe

Little, Brown and Company

New York • Boston • London

Little, Brown and Company
Hachette Book Group USA
237 Park Avenue, New York, NY 10169
Visit our Web site at www.HachetteBookGroupUSA.com

First Edition: April 2007

Library of Congress Cataloging-in-Publication Data

Brown, Katie.
   Katie Brown's outdoor entertaining : taking the party outside.
      p. cm.
Includes bibliographical references and index.
ISBN-13: 978-0-316-11306-9
ISBN-10: 0-316-11306-9
1. Entertaining. 2. Outdoor cookery. I. Title.

TX731.B76144 2007
642'.4—dc22   2006018182

Design: Gary Tooth/Empire Design Studio
Printed in Singapore by Imago

THIS BOOK IS DEDICATED TO

BOO CORBIN

KNOWN TO SOME AS BILL, WILL,
WILLY/BILLY, AND TO ME AS WILLIAM

From the moment you left the room

to the day the lines made you jump in,

I have been yours.

From the night you bravely cradled our small child

to the moment you made the show mine,

I have been yours.

Your optimism will always fill our dips and your

enthusiasm and joy will always be my light.

The best step I ever took was walking down

the aisle with you.

Thank you.

Backyard Reunion

Down by the Sea

Garden Party

Herbal Delight

Contents

Here Comes the Sun

Rustic Woods

My one favorite place in the whole entire world is my family cottage on Lake Michigan, Camp Anomanong. No matter where I travel—from India to Africa, from Colorado to New York City— it still keeps coming up number one. And you know how when you grow up and you return to places you knew as a child, they usually seem to be smaller and less grand than you remember? Not true for this camp. I will grant you, the beds are a bit hard, the kitchen could use some updating, and the bathrooms are barely civilized. But the outdoor space—the grounds, if you will—continue to delight and overwhelm me.

At age three, I remember, I was so proud of learning how to jump off the wall in our front yard. At five, I would practice my counting as I placed a foot in the center of each large stone that led to our front door. Our outdoor fireplace is where I mastered the skill of roasting marshmallows. Every summer ended with the gathering of twigs, cedar, and berries to be placed on the groups of large stones so the fairies would not go hungry.

We did and do everything outdoors at our family's gathering place—from dinners to long conversations to various plays staged in the big front lawn to great games of wiffle ball and volleyball. I would watch my aunts garden and my mother collect a bounty for the center of the table. There seemed to be no end to what we could produce in our great outdoor space. So it should come as no surprise to you that this is my inspiration, my motivation for the creation of this book.

Sure, the "outdoors in" look is here to stay, and outdoor barbecues are looking more and more like high-tech kitchens. I am interested in promoting this trend, but with a little something extra. What, you ask, could I possibly add to what Mother Nature has already delivered and appliance manufacturers have taken to new heights? Fellowship is my answer. Inspirations and ideas that will help you stage a production that will create memories for all you love and touch.

Use these pages full of projects and recipes to deliver to your family and friends your own backdrop for them to play and live with. So whether you have a whole camp, a short walkway, or an arrangement of potted plants as your outdoor space, nurture it, love it, and fill it up with the spirit of this book, and I promise young and old will remember and love it for years to come. Your outdoors, like my lakeside camp, will not shrink and age with time if you continue to take the party outside.

I come from a *very* large family—six pairs of aunts and uncles and thirty-two first cousins, to be exact.

Backyard
Reunion

With such an extended brood, it is no wonder that most of my stories relate back to memories of my family. And although we may be large in number, we are even richer in diversity; we have cousins who are bold and brave enough to run marathons through the streets of New York City, and some as timid as to have to cover their eyes when crossing the great bridge that connects the peninsulas of our home state, Michigan. We live as far away as Washington State and as close to home as our grandmother and grandfather's first house. Some earn a living by selling fish, others toil away in a bank, captain a boat, or run a ski resort.

Once a year, no matter where we may be, we manage to fly, sail, or drive our way back to our family's home on the shores of Lake Michigan. Everyone—brave, bold, timid, shy, gregarious, bragadocious, humble, awkward, backward, progressive—gathers together under the roof of our family founders, Mom and Dad Brown, who taught us the importance of reunions and how these precious occasions should be spent with the utmost togetherness.

In the great memory of Mom Brown, I developed these recipes and projects to take you outside, to cook (out of the kitchen) and entertain (away from the dining room), surrounded by birds, trees, and fresh air—a place filled with the laughter and the hugs from each and every one of your brood. So whether you are reuniting with family, getting to know your neighbors, or relaxing with your colleagues outside the office, gather together on Mother Nature's permanent picnic blanket and enjoy!

Soda Floats

Float, float — this will certainly float your boat.

....

SERVES 8

INGREDIENTS

2 pints strawberry ice cream

2 pints vanilla ice cream

1 liter lemon-lime soda

1. In chilled mugs, place one scoop of strawberry ice cream on the bottom. Top with one scoop of vanilla ice cream. (You can use any of your favorite ice cream flavors.)

2. Top off each mug with lemon-lime soda and serve immediately.

Whipped Feta
& Pesto Dip with Crudités

A tisket, a tasket, put it in a basket.

SERVES 8-10

INGREDIENTS

1 cup crumbled feta cheese

¼ cup sour cream

¼ cup mayonnaise

1 tablespoon olive oil

1 tablespoon lemon juice

½ teaspoon salt

½ teaspoon pepper

1 tablespoon prepared pesto

1. In a food processor or blender, place feta cheese, sour cream, mayonnaise, olive oil, lemon juice, salt, and pepper. Process until almost smooth.

2. Pour into a serving bowl. Stir in pesto.

3. Serve immediately, or cover and refrigerate until ready to serve.

Cold Asparagus
Crudités with Garlic Dip

Dip, dip, dip!

SERVES 8-10

INGREDIENTS

2 bunches thin asparagus

1 cup mayonnaise

2 tablespoons olive oil

1¼ cups grated Parmesan cheese

3 cloves garlic, crushed and minced

1. Place a large pot of salted water over high heat and bring to a boil.

2. While water is coming to a boil, prepare an ice bath by placing ice and cold water in a large bowl.

3. Trim the lower two-thirds of each asparagus spear. Discard any wilted spears. Add asparagus to the boiling water and cook until almost tender, 2–3 minutes. Transfer asparagus to ice bath and let cool completely. When cool, remove from ice bath and drain in a colander. Set aside.

4. To make garlic dip, place mayonnaise, olive oil, Parmesan cheese, and garlic in a food processor and process until smooth. Season to taste with salt and pepper.

Beer-simmered
Grilled Brats

Gretchen, who developed many of the recipes in this book, is from Wisconsin, where bratwursts are practically the state mascot. She even once had a T-shirt that said "I ♥ Beer Brats"!

....

SERVES 12

INGREDIENTS

One six-pack of your favorite pilsner or ale-style beer

2 large onions, cut into ½-inch slices

12 uncooked bratwursts

12 hoagie rolls or large hot dog buns

Condiments

1. In a large saucepan, combine beer, onions, and brats, and bring to a simmer, uncovered. Let simmer until brats are just cooked through, 20–30 minutes. You can simmer the brats ahead of time and store in the fridge in the beer mixture until ready to grill.

2. Prepare grill for medium heat.

3. Remove brats from beer mixture. Continue to simmer onions until they are cooked through. Remove onions and discard liquid.

4. Grill brats until nicely browned on all sides.

5. Serve brats immediately on buns with beer-simmered onions and condiments such as ketchup, mustard, pickle relish, and sauerkraut.

Cheese-stuffed
Turkey Burgers

There is always a debate among grillmasters about when to place the cheese on the burger during the grilling process. A great way to rise above the debate is to place the cheese in the center when forming the patty. Who can argue over a cheesy surprise?

....

SERVES 12

INGREDIENTS

3 pounds ground turkey

Salt and pepper

1 pound shredded Monterey Jack cheese

12 hamburger buns, split

Condiments

1. Prepare grill for medium heat.

2. Season the turkey with salt and pepper and form into two 2-inch patties. Place a scant tablespoon of cheese in the middle of one patty and top with the other patty. Gently press the edges of the patties together to create a seal. Repeat with the rest of the ground turkey to make 12 burgers.

3. Grill burgers until cooked through, approximately 5 minutes per side.

4. Serve immediately on buns with condiments.

Chipotle Mayo

We suggest serving this with your burger.

....

INGREDIENTS

1 cup mayonnaise

2 tablespoons sauce from 1 can of chipotle chilies in adobo sauce

Mix mayonnaise and sauce well in a bowl. Serve immediately, or refrigerate until ready to serve.

BBQ Chicken Drumsticks

Sometimes you want to dress it up a little bit and have something a little more special than hamburgers and hot dogs. Look no further than a chicken for your next backyard gathering.

SERVES 12

INGREDIENTS

2 tablespoons olive oil

1 cup minced onion

1 tablespoon minced garlic

1 bottle barbecue sauce

2 teaspoons yellow mustard

1 tablespoon molasses

¼ cup bourbon

24 chicken drumsticks

Salt and pepper

1. Place olive oil in a saucepan and heat over high heat. Add onion and garlic and sauté until cooked through, 4–5 minutes.

2. Add barbecue sauce, mustard, molasses, and bourbon to the onion mixture. Bring to a simmer and cook until sauce thickens, 10–15 minutes. Remove from heat and set aside. (The sauce can be made up to 3 days in advance.)

3. Season chicken drumsticks liberally with salt and pepper. Set aside.

4. Prepare grill for medium heat. Grill drumsticks, turning to cook on all sides, until skin is crisp and juices run clear, 20–30 minutes.

5. Transfer about half of the barbecue sauce to a bowl and reserve. Brush drumsticks with remaining sauce and cook until a glaze forms, another 3–4 minutes.

6. Remove drumsticks from grill and serve immediately or at room temperature along with the reserved sauce.

Corn & Tomatoes
Tossed with Blue Cheese

Grow your own or pick 'em up from your local grocer—
no matter, the yellow and red (and blue) will look great
and taste great at your outdoor picnic.

SERVES 8–10

INGREDIENTS

1 lemon, cut in half

2 tablespoons sugar

6 ears fresh corn, shucked

1 pint grape tomatoes, cut in half

1 green pepper, chopped

1 small red onion, chopped

¾ cup crumbled blue cheese

1 tablespoon chopped fresh thyme

¼ cup olive oil

¼ cup red wine vinegar

Salt and pepper

1. Add lemon and sugar to a large pot of water and bring it to a boil over high heat.

2. While water is coming to a boil, prepare an ice bath by placing ice and cold water in a large bowl.

3. Add corn to boiling water and cook until just done, 3–4 minutes. Remove from water and transfer to ice bath to stop the cooking process. Remove from ice bath. Cut corn from ears and place in a large mixing bowl. Let cool completely.

4. Add grape tomatoes, green pepper, red onion, blue cheese, thyme, olive oil, and vinegar. Toss to combine and season with salt and pepper to taste.

5. Serve immediately or cover and refrigerate until ready to serve.

Molasses & Brown
Sugar Baked Beans

My mother had a brown ceramic bean crock,
and I knew that if she pulled it out, there
was going to be a party. And somewhere there
would be plenty of ketchup!

SERVES 10

INGREDIENTS

1 (48-ounce) can pork and beans

¼ cup brown sugar

¼ cup molasses

½ cup ketchup

5 slices bacon, cooked and chopped

½ teaspoon dry mustard

½ cup chopped onion

1. Preheat oven to 350 degrees.

2. Combine all ingredients in a large bowl and pour into a casserole dish. Cover with foil and bake for 30 minutes.

3. Uncover and bake for another 20–30 minutes.

Mixed Berry
& Pound Cake Trifle

This is a great way to dress up a store-bought staple with a summertime treat of fresh berries.

....

SERVES 6

INGREDIENTS

1 pint strawberries, quartered

1 pint raspberries

1 pint blueberries

2 tablespoons sugar

¼ cup chopped mint

1 pint heavy cream

1 tablespoon confectioners' sugar

1 teaspoon vanilla extract

1 prepared pound cake, cut into 1-inch slices

1. Combine all berries with sugar and mint. Toss lightly and set aside.

2. Whip heavy cream with confectioners' sugar and vanilla until fluffy. Set aside.

3. In dessert glasses or cardboard French fry containers, place a layer of berries on the bottom. Top with cake, then whipped cream. Place another layer of cake on top of whipped cream and top with berries.

Chilled Watermelon

Slices with Lime Juice, Honey, & Mint

You wouldn't think you could make this Mother Nature specialty any better, but I promise, a dose of lime juice, honey, and mint will bring out the best she has to offer.

··

SERVES 10-12

INGREDIENTS

1 watermelon, chilled and sliced

½ cup fresh lime juice

Zest from one lime

¼ cup honey

½ cup chopped mint

1. Place watermelon slices on a decorative platter.

2. In a small bowl, whisk together lime juice, zest, and honey.

3. Drizzle lime juice mixture over slices of watermelon. Sprinkle mint on top and serve immediately.

Billy Goat Cookies

Combine everything you ever tried to sneak from the pantry when you were a kid, bake it, and watch the children grin with a knowing smile.

MAKES 2 DOZEN COOKIES

INGREDIENTS

1 package chocolate-chip cookie mix

½ cup chopped walnuts

½ cup flaked coconut

½ cup white chocolate chips

½ cup peanut butter chips

1. Preheat oven as directed on cookie mix package. Grease two cookie sheets.

2. Make cookie dough according to package instructions. Fold in walnuts, coconut, white chocolate chips, and peanut butter chips.

3. Drop by rounded teaspoonfuls an inch apart onto cookie sheets and bake according to package directions.

Painted Tabletop

One less step for setting your table—no need for linens or flimsy plastic table covers. This tabletop will last year after year.

....

MATERIALS

¾-inch plywood, 4 x 8 feet (standard size)

2 quarts exterior paint, 2 shades of red

Painter's tape

2 sawhorses

TOOLS

Paintbrush or small roller

Measuring tape

Pencil

● Paint the plywood in thick bands of color in either direction.

● Prop your table on sawhorses or bales of hay for a fun, down-home barbecue feel.

● Make it last summer after summer by adding a coat of varnish on top.

Food Covers

There is nothing better than an outdoor family feast, but nothing will *bug* you more than your food being enjoyed by bugs. Keep them out politely with these bug-be-gone burlap covers.

....

MATERIALS

Colored burlap

Wooden beads (2 colors)

TOOLS

Scissors

• Cut burlap squares a bit wider than your bowls.

• Fringe the edges, and slide wooden beads onto the burlap strands all the way around.

• Either knot the fringe or add a dab of glue to keep the bead secure.

• The weight of the beaded trim will keep the covers in place and the bugs out of the food.

BBQ Baskets

**Make outdoor eating easier with these
dressed-up food baskets.**

MATERIALS

Bandannas

Small wicker baskets

Wax paper

TOOLS

Pinking shears

● Cut and tie strips of bandanna
around a lunchbox-size wicker
basket.

● Line it with wax paper, and there
you have it—food that not only tastes
good but looks good, too.

Brown Bag Burgers

Keep your fixin's on the bun with these burger bags.

MATERIALS

**Brown lunch bags
(smaller sizes available
at craft stores)**

Sponge

**Stamp pads in red,
white and blue**

TOOLS

Scissors

Pen

Pinking shears

● Cut small sandwich bags in half.

● Add decorative homemade stamps
in fun shapes. Stamps can be made
out of many household items—sponges,
potatoes, apples, you name it.

Pails of Pop

Yes, *pop*. I know, it sounds like a word from another era. But where I'm from, in northern Michigan, it describes every sweet, bubbly drink. Here's my solution to the eternal search for the lost bottle opener.

MATERIALS

Bottle opener

12-inch section of metal chain

Galvanized bucket

2 key rings

Strong magnet

Floral wire

Small sunflowers or Gerber daisies

TOOLS

Wire cutters

● Attach an opener to the end of a chain and fasten it to a bucket with a simple key ring.

● Go one step further and add a magnet so the bottle opener is always in place.

● We thought the drinks seemed a little lonely, so we dressed up their home with some wired flowers.

Tin Planters

**Make your homegrown crop stylish this summer
by hammering tin tiles onto basic wooden planters.**

MATERIALS

Wood crates

Tin ceiling tiles

Heavy-duty garbage bags

Tape

Large upholstery tacks

TOOLS

Tin snips

Hammer

Protective gloves

● Convert your slatted crate into a planter by first lining the inside with a heavy-duty garbage bag. Use tape to hold the bag in place.

● Tin is a cinch to cut and will look great when attached with decorative upholstery tacks.

● Cut tin squares to a size that you can fold over the lip of the crate. Hammer in place with upholstery tacks.

● Make it chic by giving your planters a centerpiece: create a fountain with a half-barrel and a simple fountain pump.

● Crates are available at craft stores such as Michael's; tin ceiling tiles are available online at www.americantinceilings.com.

zucchini and summer squash

tomatoes

bell peppers

red and white cabbage

Gardens-a-Plenty

When you grow your own veggies, do you end up with more than you bargained for? Well, I say gather the neighbors, call up your family, and dig in!

IDEAS

Tomatoes

Bell peppers

Cucumbers

Green beans

Snap peas

Summer squash

Lettuce

Spinach

GARDENING TIPS

❧ Start seedlings inside. Before transplanting, water the seedlings well. Transplants come in plastic flats called six-packs. To remove them from their cells, turn the flat upside down and lightly tap the bottom with one hand. The plants and soil should pop out easily. If the plants do not slip out easily, simply break the plastic away from the root ball.

❧ Transplant plants outdoors once the threat of frost is over. Place individual plants in the ground, firming the soil around the base of each plant.

❧ Use time-released fertilizer for stronger, healthier plants.

❧ Tomatoes, beans, and some cucumber varieties need staking to provide support for the lengthy branches. Beans and peas need to be harvested regularly when they're coming on or else the plant will go to seed. The little effort you spend will be rewarded with an abundance of lush, healthy vegetables.

❧ When planting in containers, water diligently. A plant's root system can't grow as deeply in a container, so the plant's success depends on regular watering and care.

❧ Use "determinant"-variety vegetables, which mature to a size appropriate to the container.

ENAMELED STEEL TOP FOR PICK OF CROP

What would the great outdoors
be without the gift of the sea?

Down by
the Sea

The mother of all life and the muse to countless artists from Turner to Debussy, from Frost to Wyeth, from Sugimoto to Gordon Lightfoot? Hemingway, Melville, and Fitzgerald all have a debt to the sea for inspiring some of their best work. So who would I be when creating my own humble nod to the natural world that surrounds us without giving it up to the vast open sea of blue?

I am eternally grateful for the sea from three perspectives: First, as an individual who harvests relaxation from the sounds, sights, and smells—the peace that comes from taking a nice deep breath of ocean air, the sea breeze that settles our souls, and the rhythm that lures us into relaxation when the tides ebb and flow. Second, as a mother who loves to watch her young daughter joyously explore the sand and the waves—hearing my daughter's giggle as she tickles her toes through the sand has been one of my greatest delights of motherhood. And third as a home designer and cook who searches for inspiration in every possible environment. I revel in the designs of seashells, the soft texture of the sand, the relaxing sounds of the water, and the great variety and lightness in seafood flavors. Even with all my admiration, I am appropriately intimidated by this most powerful attribute of the great outdoors. I am respectful of the sea's might and humbled by her wrath; she is a complicated wonder but a wonder nonetheless.

So, I say, embrace this natural phenomenon by contemplating this chapter. Whether you have the luxury of spending a day seaside or simply the motivation to re-create some of her characteristics, these next pages will hopefully lead you toward a reverence to all things that the great blue expanse yields.

Passion Fruit Sangria

Sitting in your backyard sipping this refreshment, close
your eyes and let the tropical flavors of this concoction
take you to the shores of the most exotic beaches.

SERVES 8–10

INGREDIENTS

One 12-ounce can
passion fruit nectar

1 cup orange juice

2 bottles dry
white wine

1 cup brandy

¼ cup orange liqueur

¼ cup confectioners'
sugar

1 orange, sliced

2 limes, sliced

1 cup fresh mint
leaves

1. Combine passion fruit nectar,
orange juice, wine, brandy,
orange liqueur, and confectioners'
sugar in a large pitcher. Cover
and refrigerate until chilled.

2. Garnish with fruit slices and
mint leaves and serve over ice.

Tomato-rubbed
Flat Bread

My sister Lynn and her family lived in Spain for a year and haven't stopped talking about it since. This easy-to-make, easy-to-eat side dish is a traditional Catalan favorite. How can tomatoes and bread taste this good?

SERVES 6–8

INGREDIENTS

One 28-ounce can whole plum tomatoes, drained

4 cloves garlic, chopped

½ teaspoon dried oregano

1 teaspoon cumin

Sea salt and pepper

1 package pita bread (6 pieces)

½ cup cilantro, chopped

1. Preheat broiler or grill pan.

2. In a food processor or blender, combine tomatoes, garlic, oregano, cumin, a pinch of salt, and a pinch of pepper, and puree until smooth.

3. Split pitas in half horizontally and place cut side up on a broiler plate.

4. Place pita halves under broiler or on hot grill pan. Broil or grill until brown (watch them closely, as they will burn quickly).

5. Brush tomato puree onto each pita, sprinkle with cilantro, and serve.

Seared Tuna Salad
with Avocado &
Jalapeño Vinaigrette

Seafood and greens — nothing says beachfront better than that.

....

SERVES 10

INGREDIENTS

Salad

Four 8-ounce tuna steaks, about 1 inch thick

2 tablespoons olive oil, plus 1 tablespoon olive oil for brushing

Salt and pepper

2 limes, cut in half

3 bags ready-to-use mixed baby greens

2 firm but ripe avocados, peeled, pitted, and diced

1 pint cherry or grape tomatoes, sliced in half

Vinaigrette

1 jalapeño, seeded and chopped

½ cup cilantro leaves, chopped

1 scallion, chopped

1 garlic clove, chopped

1 teaspoon cumin

¼ cup red wine vinegar

½ cup olive oil

Salt and pepper

1. Heat grill or grill pan to medium heat (if using a grill pan, coat with 2 tablespoons olive oil).

2. Lightly brush tuna steaks on both sides with 1 tablespoon olive oil. Generously season tuna fillets on both sides with salt and pepper. When grill or grill pan is hot, add tuna steaks and sear. When a nice brown crust forms on one side, turn over and sear until tuna is slightly opaque in the center. Remove from heat, squeeze limes over tuna, and let cool. Flake tuna coarsely and set aside.

3. Place mixed greens in a large bowl.

4. Combine all vinaigrette ingredients in a food processor and puree until smooth.

5. Drizzle half the vinaigrette over greens and toss to combine. Top tossed greens with avocados, tomatoes, and chopped tuna, and then drizzle remaining vinaigrette over the top and serve.

Grilled Red Snapper
with Ginger Marinade

My husband considers himself the grillmaster of all of New York. He tinkers, he toys, he spices, he sizzles— so, needless to say, he was my taste tester for this gift from the sea.

SERVES 10

INGREDIENTS

Marinade

¼ cup freshly grated ginger

3 cloves garlic, chopped

½ cup lime juice

Zest of 2 limes

½ cup chopped scallions

½ cup chopped parsley

½ cup olive oil

Salt and pepper

Red Snapper

Ten 6-ounce red snapper fillets, skin on and deboned

Olive oil for brushing

Salt and pepper

Lime wedges for garnish

1. Combine all marinade ingredients in a food processor and puree until smooth.

2. Place snapper fillets in one layer in a 13 x 9-inch glass baking dish. Spread marinade over fillets. Cover and refrigerate 20–30 minutes.

3. In the meantime, prepare the grill for medium-high heat.

4. Remove snapper fillets from marinade and shake off excess. Season fillets with a pinch of salt and pepper. Place skin side down on grill. Grill until the skin is nicely browned and crispy and turn to finish cooking. Remove from grill when fillets are just cooked through, 3–4 minutes per side.

5. Garnish with lime wedges and serve immediately.

Grilled Jerk Shrimp Skewers with Watermelon Salsa

A trip to Jamaica would cost you a pretty penny, but this Caribbean dish will only cost you a trip to the grocery store.

....

SERVES 10

INGREDIENTS

Skewers

¼ cup olive oil

¼ cup orange juice

3 tablespoons Jamaican jerk or Caribbean spice blend

40 jumbo shrimp, deveined and shelled

Salsa

4 cups watermelon, seeded and diced

2 jalapeño peppers, seeded and finely diced

½ cup fresh lime juice

Zest from 2 limes

2 tablespoons honey

½ cup cilantro leaves, chopped

¾ cup finely chopped scallion

½ inch ginger root, peeled and finely grated

Salt and pepper

1. Combine olive oil, orange juice, and spice in a large bowl. Add shrimp and toss to coat. Let marinate for 20–30 minutes.

2. Meanwhile, combine all ingredients for watermelon salsa. Cover and refrigerate. Salsa can be prepared up to 2 hours in advance.

3. Preheat grill for medium-high heat.

4. Remove shrimp from marinade and place four shrimp on each skewer. Season shrimp with salt and pepper. Grill until just cooked through, 2–3 minutes on each side.

5. Serve skewers with salsa on the side.

SPECIAL EQUIPMENT

10 wooden skewers, soaked in water for 1 hour

My Mom's
Planked Whitefish

Growing up in Michigan, we used to frequent a restaurant called Juilleret's. They served a fish that was so good that my mother sweet-talked the chef into telling her how it was done. Lucky for you, here it is!

SERVES 4

INGREDIENTS

2 tablespoons olive oil

1 lemon cut in half

1 fillet whitefish

1 tablespoon paprika

2 scallions, thinly sliced

2 tablespoons butter, cut into 8 pieces

1. Prepare the grill for medium heat.

2. Spread olive oil on plank and squeeze juice of one half lemon over the oil.

3. Lay whitefish on oiled plank and top with paprika and scallions. Squeeze juice of other half lemon on top. Place pats of butter along the top of the fish, about 3 inches apart.

4. Place plank on the grill and cook until fish segments separate, about 20 minutes.

SPECIAL EQUIPMENT
Wooden plank (cedar, maple, or hemlock) soaked in water for 2 hours

Creamy Coconut
& Cilantro Rice

I can't get enough of cilantro — so much so that I wish it would last in my fridge forever. Here's a tip: Put the cilantro with the stems down in a cup of water, cover with a plastic bag, and refrigerate. Freshen the water every few days and your zesty herb will last up to two weeks.

SERVES 10

INGREDIENTS

2 cups unsweetened coconut milk, stirred well

1 cup low-sodium chicken broth

Salt

3 cups long-grain rice, rinsed and drained

1 cup cilantro leaves, chopped

1. In a saucepan set over medium heat, bring coconut milk, chicken broth, and a dash of salt to a boil.

2. Reduce heat to low and add rice. Cover and simmer until most of liquid is absorbed.

3. Remove from heat, stir in cilantro, and let rice stand, covered, until liquid is completely absorbed and rice is tender.

Corn & Pepper Jack
Fry Cakes

A fish fry, a clam bake — or how about some savory, flavorful corn cakes?

SERVES 8

INGREDIENTS

4 tablespoons olive oil

2 cups canned corn, drained

½ red bell pepper, seeded and finely chopped

½ cup chopped onion

1 clove garlic, minced

1 cup cornmeal

1 cup flour

1 teaspoon baking soda

½ teaspoon salt

¼ teaspoon cayenne pepper

1 cup grated Pepper Jack cheese

2 cups buttermilk

4 eggs

1. Heat 2 tablespoons olive oil in a large sauté pan over high heat. Add corn, red pepper, onion, and garlic. Sauté over high heat until corn starts to brown and red pepper and onion are tender, about 5 minutes. Remove from heat, and cool completely.

2. In a large bowl, combine cornmeal, flour, baking soda, salt, and cayenne pepper. Stir in cooled vegetable mixture and cheese.

3. In another bowl, whisk together buttermilk and eggs until well blended. Add to the vegetable mixture and mix until just combined.

4. Heat 2 tablespoons olive oil in a large nonstick sauté pan over medium-high heat. Drop in batter by scant ¼-cupfuls and cook until golden brown on both sides, about 2 minutes per side. Serve warm.

Curried
Potato Salad

There are infinite ways to dress a potato, and this uniquely strong combination of flavors is a perfect accompaniment to any seaside menu.

SERVES 8

INGREDIENTS

2 pounds baby new potatoes, cut in half

1 cup mayonnaise

½ cup sour cream

2 tablespoons Dijon mustard

2 teaspoons cumin

1 teaspoon ground coriander

½ teaspoon ground turmeric

1 bunch scallions, chopped

2 jalapeños, seeded and minced

2 ribs celery, chopped

Salt and pepper

1. Place a large pot of salted water over high heat and add potatoes. Bring to a boil and cook, uncovered, until potatoes are just tender (do not overcook).

2. Meanwhile, combine mayonnaise, sour cream, mustard, and spices in a small bowl and mix until well blended. Set aside.

3. Drain potatoes and place in a large bowl. Add scallions, jalapeños, and celery. Pour dressing over potatoes while they are still warm and mix well. Season with salt and pepper to taste. Serve at room temperature, or cover and chill until needed. This can be made two days ahead.

Easy
Vanilla Bean Flan

A clean, light, elegant dessert.

SERVES 12

INGREDIENTS

1 cup sugar

12 prepared miniature graham cracker crusts

Two 14-ounce cans sweetened condensed milk

6 eggs

6 egg yolks

1 vanilla bean, split, or 1 teaspoon vanilla extract

1. Preheat oven to 325 degrees.

2. In a heavy saucepan, combine sugar and 1 tablespoon water and bring to a boil over medium heat. Continue to boil until it becomes amber in color. Remove from heat and carefully pour melted sugar into prepared crusts (be careful when pouring this mixture, as it is very hot). Set aside.

3. In a blender, combine sweetened condensed milk, eggs, egg yolks, and vanilla and mix until well blended. Fill each crust three-quarters full. Place flans on a baking sheet and bake until the centers are set, 30–40 minutes.

Seashells
on the Seashore

This will be one of the more intricate projects you
will undertake, but you will be so glad that you did.
It will survive the seasons year after year and never
look outdated. Sit under your umbrella and enjoy
the delicate sound of the clinking sand dollars—a
classic and elegant achievement.

....

MATERIALS

Patio umbrella

**32-inch round plastic
planter with tray**

Plastic spray primer

Off-white spray paint

Umbrella stand

Ceramic tile adhesive

Sand dollars

Small starfish

Scallop shells

**Premixed sanded grout
or fine-grain sand mixed
with plain grout.**

Grout sealer

Insulating foam

Sisal fisherman's throw net

Large conch shell (optional)

Zip-locking plastic bag

TOOLS

Drill

Heavy-duty knife

Spatula

Scissors

STAND BASE

● Measure the diameter of the umbrella
pole and, with the drill, punch a concen-
tric circle of holes in the center of the
planter's tray slightly larger than the
pole's diameter. With the knife, punch
out the circle.

● Spray primer on the plastic planter,
let dry for 1 hour, and then cover
completely with off-white spray paint.

● Place the umbrella stand in the
bottom of the planter and fit the planter's
tray upside down in the planter's opening.
It should fit snugly on the top of the
planter's opening. (All planters are
different, so play with yours to see how
it fits best.)

● Fill the ridge of the tray with insulating foam up to the edge of the ridge. Let
dry. The foam will expand upon drying,
and if it ends up rising above the surface
of the tray, trim it after it is dry.

● Working in small patches, thinly
cover the surface of the tray, including
the foam, with ceramic tile adhesive.
Arrange starfish and scallop shells close
together. Around the outer rim, attach
sand dollars. Let this dry for 24 hours in
a cool, dry place.

● Using a spatula or paint mixing stick,
scoop sanded grout into the plastic bag,
and seal. Cut a small hole in a corner of
the bag. Squeeze grout between shells as
if you were icing a cake. Make sure to
fill in all gaps.

● After the grout is dry and sealed,
insert the umbrella into the stand.

UMBRELLA DÉCOR

● Cut four pieces of sisal net, each sized
to reach from one edge of the umbrella
to the other.

● Lay the cut nets over the top of the
umbrella, securing them at the umbrella's point.

● Cut slits in the net at the edges all
the way around the umbrella and attach
sand dollars by slipping the sisal through
the hole in the sand dollar and tying it.

● Attach a large conch shell over the
top point of the umbrella for a special
added touch.

You can buy sea shells of all shapes, sizes,
and varieties from www.seashellcity.com.
You can purchase fishnet by the yard in many
sizes and materials at www.looseends.com

Tic-Tac-Toe,
Beach-style

Board games don't have to exist only on your kitchen table! Treat the kids to an adorable outdoor surprise with this tic-tac-toe table. In the grass, on the beach, or on the patio, this will certainly bring you a lot of hugs (O's) and kisses (X's)!

MATERIALS

White outdoor paint

24 x 24 x 1-inch wood board

Four 4 x 4 x 1-inch wood legs

1 roll sisal rope

Sea glass

5 round recessed craft-wood plaques

5 square recessed craft-wood plaques

TOOLS

Paintbrush

Hot glue gun

Scissors

● Paint the game board and legs with the white outdoor paint.

● Glue four pieces of rope to the board to create the game board.

● For the game pieces, keep with the beach theme and hot-glue sea glass to small craft-wood plaques. You can differentiate between X's and O's by using different-colored sea glass or different-shaped wood plaques.

● For a more finished look, attach short wooden legs, and glue rope around the border.

Cape Cod 2001

Bridgehampton New York 2005

Cayman Islands 2000

Hilton Head, South Carolina 1996

Beach Reflections

Close your eyes, and you can hear the sounds of the ocean and feel the sand between your toes. You wish you could bottle the smells, the sounds, and the sights from your time spent near the water. Preserve it all in this very modern and minimal wall décor.

MATERIALS

Frames

Sand

Spray adhesive

Pen

Window mats

- Remove the glass from a picture frame and affix sand from a favorite vacation spot to the frame panel with spray adhesive.

- Let dry and shake off the excess sand.

- Write the name of the vacation spot on the matboard. Replace the glass cover.

- Do this for as many vacation locales as you like.

A Frosted Glow

Nothing sets a softer mood than a candle's flicker under the moonlight. Create a pathway with these lawn globes, or line them up along your front stairs for a soft and subtle glow.

MATERIALS

**Painter's tape,
1-inch wide**

Glass fishbowl vases

Newspaper

Rubber gloves

Etching cream

Sand

Pillar candle

- Using painter's tape, stripe a fishbowl vase.

- Cover your work area with newspapers. Wearing rubber gloves, apply etching cream on the clean glass, following the manufacturer's instructions.

- Fill the bowl almost halfway with sand and insert the pillar candle.

Sounds of the Sea

I've noticed a trend in my life: I always live near a large body of water. Water relaxes and inspires me, and it certainly inspired this lovely backyard fountain.

MATERIALS

Flexible banboo fencing

Wooden planter

U-shaped nails

Heavy-duty pond liner

Fountain pump

Heavy rock

Thick bamboo pole, cut

4 thin bamboo rods

TOOLS

Wire cutters

Hammer

Staple gun

- Wrap flexible bamboo fencing around a wooden planter, attaching it with U-shaped nails.

- Waterproof the inside of the planter with a pond liner. Fill with water and place a fountain pump in the bottom (a heavy rock is great for keeping it in place).

- Cover the fountain spigot with a piece of wider bamboo, and crisscross thin bamboo stalks across the edges of the fountain for added decoration. Bamboo is simple to cut, especially with a razor saw.

Floating Flora

It's hard not to be amazed by the fluidity of floating water plants. It seems almost impossible that they can live without roots in the ground. All you need is a container and water—no soil, no tools, no gardening gloves. And all three of these plants live well in containers.

PLANTS

Water hyacinths

Water lettuce

Fairy moss

TIPS

❧ Containers get heavy when they're full of water, so assemble the pot in its permanent location. Choose a spot that gets full sun for at least five hours a day.

❧ Water gardens are very low-maintenance—they take care of themselves as long as you keep adding fresh water.

❧ Keep your eyes peeled for algae. Mosquitoes are attracted to it and will eat your plants. Consider dropping mosquito pellets into the water to keep the water bug-free.

❧ Pond pots, or "still pots," work well in small spaces such as balconies or decks. All you need is a small nondraining, nonporous pot and a water plant.

Ladies who lunch . . .
oh, to be a lady who lunches!

Garden **Party**

It conjures up images of a woman whose dresses are always expertly cleaned and pressed, never one who has to endure the struggle of having three different wardrobe sizes and trying to decide whether she is of the small, medium, or large variety that day. Or to be a lady who never cancels a workout, who heads straight to the manicurist at the first sign of a chipped nail. Mostly I want to be a lady who lunches because of the girlfriend companionship.

As a busy working mom I miss the comradery that comes with female bonding—the compassion that only a fellow female can feel when describing the challenges of womanhood, the hints and secrets that can be revealed only through the conversations of girls. Their femininity and manners make me raise my game; I find myself mimicking a gesture, a look, or an accessory of a fellow diner. I eavesdrop on several conversations in order to be in touch with all the new tips and trends; I watch as these women walk effortlessly in what appears to be unmanageable heels, and I aspire to achieve the same with the purchase of my next footwear item.

As I prepare for a female celebration, I contemplate how to create a setting that can get the most out of my fellow diners. What in my tabletop will encourage their female intuition to come tumbling out so that all involved will leave with a newfound love of all things womanly? First set the party outside where the lighting is flattering to all. Next, embrace the color that is oh so female, **PINK.** Then when awakening overworked fellow flowers, highlight the delicacy of flowers themselves by preparing favors and centerpieces that accentuate their beauty and remind your guests of their own power for pleasure, and do it simply and effortlessly in the always festive backdrop of the great outdoors.

Katie's Grasshopper

This drink is like mint ice cream through a straw. I can't imagine anything more refreshing!

....

SERVES 4

INGREDIENTS

2 pints vanilla bean ice cream

½ cup milk

3 tablespoons crème de menthe

Shaved chocolate for garnish

1. Combine ice cream, milk, and crème de menthe in a blender and process until smooth.

2. Pour into four tall glasses and garnish with shaved chocolate. Serve immediately.

Crab Dip Crostini

Hammering and cracking crabs might appear quite unladylike at your afternoon fete. Here is the perfect resolution so you can have your crab and eat it, too.

....

SERVES 8–10

INGREDIENTS

1 baguette, cut into 1-inch-thick slices

Olive oil

Salt

½ cup cream cheese, room temperature

2 tablespoons mayonnaise

2 tablespoons heavy cream

1 teaspoon salt

½ teaspoon cayenne pepper

2 green onions, chopped

½ cup chopped red bell pepper

1 tablespoon lemon juice

1 tablespoon chopped parsley

Two 6-ounce cans jumbo lump crabmeat, drained

1. Preheat broiler.

2. On a cookie sheet, line up baguette slices. Brush lightly with olive oil and season with a sprinkling of salt.

3. Place baguette slices under the broiler and broil until golden brown. Flip slices over and broil until golden brown. Remove and let cool on a rack.

4. In a large mixing bowl, mix cream cheese, mayonnaise, heavy cream, salt, cayenne pepper, green onions, red bell pepper, lemon juice, and parsley. Stir to combine completely. Add crabmeat and toss lightly.

5. Spoon crab mixture onto toasted baguette slices. Serve immediately.

Tapenade &
Prosciutto Puffs

Frozen puff pastry is like magic. You will hear repeatedly, "You made these?!"

MAKES 20-25 PUFFS

INGREDIENTS

One 15-ounce can pitted black or green olives

1–2 anchovy fillets

1 tablespoon chopped garlic

2 tablespoons chopped fresh thyme (or 1 tablespoon dried thyme)

¼ cup extra-virgin olive oil

Salt and pepper

¼ pound prosciutto

1 package puff sheets, thawed

1 egg beaten with 1 tablespoon water for an egg wash

1. Preheat oven to 400 degrees.

2. In a food processor, combine olives, anchovies, garlic, and thyme and process until finely chopped. While the processor is running, drizzle in olive oil and process until incorporated. (The tapenade will still be slightly chunky.) Season with salt and pepper. As a time saver, you can purchase tapenade at your neighborhood grocery store.

3. On a lightly floured surface, roll out puff pastry sheets to about ⅛ inch thick. Cut out circles with a round cookie cutter. Place half of the circles on a cookie sheet.

4. Place a small piece of prosciutto on each circle on the cookie sheet and top with a teaspoon of tapenade. Brush the edges of the circle with egg wash, place another circle on top, and press the puff pastry edges to seam. Brush egg wash over each turnover.

5. Bake for 20-25 minutes, until puffed and golden brown.

6. Let cool on a rack for 10 minutes. Serve warm or at room temperature.

Quick Spoon Biscuits with Goat Cheese & Chives

These are quick to bake and even quicker to eat—and it's impossible to eat just one.

MAKES 8 BISCUITS

INGREDIENTS

2 cups all-purpose flour

1 tablespoon baking powder

1½ teaspoons salt

½ teaspoon baking soda

5 tablespoons cold unsalted butter

1½ cups crumbled fresh goat cheese

3 tablespoons chives, chopped

1 cup buttermilk

1. Preheat oven to 425 degrees. Grease a cookie sheet.

2. Whisk together flour, baking powder, salt, and baking soda in a large bowl. Cut in butter with a pastry blender or your fingertips until the mixture resembles coarse meal. Add goat cheese, chives, and buttermilk and stir until just combined (do not overmix).

3. Drop batter in eight equal mounds about 2 inches apart on the prepared cookie sheet.

4. Bake until golden brown, 10 to 12 minutes, and cool on the cookie sheets.

Spinach & Artichoke Salad Pizza

With this pizza, you can say you had a salad for lunch!

SERVES 8

INGREDIENTS

2 prepared pizza crusts

One 5-ounce bag ready-to-use baby spinach, roughly chopped

½ cup basil leaves, chopped

1 small red onion, finely chopped

½ cup cherry tomatoes, sliced thin

One 10-ounce can marinated artichoke hearts, chopped

1 tablespoon marinated artichoke oil, reserved from the can of artichoke hearts

1 tablespoon olive oil

2 tablespoons red wine vinegar

Salt and pepper

One 8-ounce package herbed cheese spread

1. Place pizza crusts on a baking sheet and bake according to package directions. Set aside to cool.

2. In a large bowl, combine spinach, basil, onion, cherry tomatoes, and artichokes. Set aside.

3. To make salad dressing, whisk together marinated artichoke oil, olive oil, and vinegar. Season with salt and pepper to taste. Drizzle over salad and toss to coat.

4. When crusts are completely cool, spread herbed cheese on them, and top with spinach salad. Slice and serve.

"Not-So-Tea"
Sandwiches

An all-girls lunch just isn't complete without the dainty addition of finger sandwiches — two bites per serving, and no one will notice if you eat them right off the buffet table.

Herby Mayo Shrimp Sandwiches

SERVES 8

INGREDIENTS

1 cup mayonnaise

2 tablespoons parsley, chopped

2 tablespoons chives, chopped

1 teaspoon tarragon, chopped

1 tablespoon fresh lemon juice

Salt and pepper

½ pound cooked medium shrimp, chopped coarsely

2 celery ribs, chopped finely

8 thin slices pumpernickel sandwich bread, crusts removed

1. Combine mayonnaise, parsley, chives, tarragon, lemon juice, and a pinch of salt and pepper to make herb mayonnaise.

2. Mix half of herb mayonnaise with shrimp and celery. Set other half aside. Cover shrimp salad and refrigerate.

3. Spread reserved herb mayonnaise on all 8 slices of bread. Top 4 slices with shrimp salad and then with the other 4 slices of bread. Cut sandwiches in half either horizontally or diagonally.

Green Vegetable Sandwiches

SERVES 8

INGREDIENTS

8 thin slices pumpernickel sandwich bread, crusts removed

1 seedless cucumber, peeled and cut into thin slices

1 avocado, peeled, pitted, and cut into ¼-inch-thick slices

½ head romaine lettuce, chopped coarsely

One 8-ounce container prepared hummus

1. Top 4 slices of bread with cucumber, avocado, and chopped lettuce.

2. Spread a thin layer of hummus on remaining 4 slices of bread. Place on top of other slices. Cut sandwiches in half either horizontally or diagonally.

Green Bean,
Garbanzo & Cherry Tomato Salad

Chickpeas for an afternoon with your favorite chicks!

....

SERVES 8

INGREDIENTS

Salad

1 pound fresh green beans, ends trimmed

1 pint cherry tomatoes, halved

One 15-ounce can garbanzo beans (chickpeas), drained and rinsed

½ cup capers, drained

½ cup pitted kalamata olives, chopped coarsely

½ cup diced red onion

2 scallions, chopped

½ cup feta cheese, crumbled

Salt and pepper

Vinaigrette

2 tablespoons olive oil

2 tablespoons fresh lemon juice

1 tablespoon Dijon mustard

1 tablespoon chopped dill

Salt and pepper

1. Place a large pot of salted water over high heat and bring to a boil.

2. While the water is coming to a boil, prepare an ice bath by placing ice and cold water in a large bowl.

3. Place green beans in the boiling water and cook until just tender. Remove immediately from boiling water and dunk into an ice bath to stop the cooking process. Let cool completely in ice bath. Remove and drain in a colander.

4. To make the vinaigrette, whisk together olive oil, lemon juice, Dijon mustard, and dill. Season with salt and pepper.

5. In a large bowl, combine green beans, cherry tomatoes, garbanzo beans, capers, olives, red onion, scallions, and feta cheese. Pour in the vinaigrette and toss. Salad can be made 1 hour ahead and chilled or served at room temperature. Add salt and pepper to taste.

Spicy Turkey Sausage
Skewers over Tossed Arugula

**Spicy sausage patties over bitter, peppery arugula —
a sophisticated and exciting flavor combo.**

SERVES 8

INGREDIENTS

Sausages

1 pound ground turkey

½ red bell pepper, diced

¼ cup parsley, chopped

2 cloves garlic, chopped

**1 teaspoon crushed red
pepper flakes**

1 teaspoon salt

1 teaspoon black pepper

½ teaspoon nutmeg

1 egg, beaten

**2 tablespoons
vegetable oil**

Tossed Arugula

2 tablespoons olive oil

1 lemon, zest and juice

Salt and pepper

**4 large bunches arugula,
trimmed of large stems**

1. In a large bowl, combine turkey, red bell pepper, parsley, garlic, red pepper flakes, salt, pepper, nutmeg, and egg. Mix gently, being careful not to overwork the ground turkey meat. Form scant ¼ cups of mixture into ½-inch-thick patties. Set aside.

2. Heat vegetable oil in a heavy large skillet over high heat. When oil is shimmering, drop in turkey patties and brown on both sides, about 4 minutes per side. Do this step in batches if necessary, to avoid overcrowding. Turkey sausages are cooked when they are firm to the touch and no longer pink in the middle. Remove sausage patties from skillet and transfer to a platter or baking sheet lined with paper towels. Place each sausage at the end of a skewer.

3. While the sausage is cooking, make a vinaigrette by whisking together olive oil, lemon zest, and lemon juice, and season to taste with salt and pepper.

4. To serve, toss arugula and vinaigrette together in a large bowl. Lay the skewered turkey sausages around the top edges of the tossed salad and serve. Make sure the sausages are not too hot or they will wilt the arugula.

Strawberry, Green Grape, & Goat Cheese Salad
with Shallot Vinaigrette

A very sophisticated twist on the traditional fruit salad.

SERVES 8

INGREDIENTS

Vinaigrette

1 shallot, minced

1 tablespoon olive oil

2 tablespoons red wine vinegar

Salt and pepper

Salad

1 pint strawberries, hulled and cut into quarters

1 cup green grapes, cut in half lengthwise

½ cup crumbled goat cheese

1. For the vinaigrette, whisk shallot, olive oil, and red wine vinegar in a small bowl. Season with salt and pepper. Set aside.

2. Place strawberries, green grapes, and goat cheese in a large bowl. Drizzle with vinaigrette and toss lightly to combine. Serve immediately.

Layered
Ice Cream Cake

I scream, you scream, we all scream for ice cream! Three layers of it, in fact.

....

SERVES 8

INGREDIENTS

1½ pints raspberry sorbet, softened

1½ pints vanilla ice cream, softened

1½ pints strawberry ice cream, softened

1. Line a bread pan with smooth foil, leaving a 1–2-inch overlap of foil around the edges.

2. Spread raspberry sorbet evenly in the bottom of the pan. Freeze for 30 minutes.

3. Spread vanilla ice cream evenly over the raspberry layer. Freeze for 30 minutes.

4. Top the vanilla layer with an even layer of strawberry ice cream. Freeze for at least 4 hours or overnight.

5. To remove the layered ice cream cake from the pan, use the foil as an aid. Gently lift the cake out of the pan. Peel the foil away. Slice and serve immediately.

A Pink Persuasion

You're throwing a party, inviting your friends and family, so invite them in a way that will make them stop in their tracks. Don't just send a mass e-mail; send something special in the mail.

MATERIALS

Ribbon

Wooden or cardboard boxes with lids

Artificial flowers

TOOLS

Glue gun

Scissors

Wire cutters

● Simply hot-glue a pink ribbon around the rim of the top to a small box, then hot-glue an artificial flower on top.

● Place your written or typed invitation inside the box. This will entice your guests to mark the date on their calendars with *ink*.

● Consider typing the party details on a label and attaching it to the back of a colorful flower seed pack.

In the Lap of Luxury

This is the perfect dressed-up tray—natural raw materials woven with the fancy touch of a ribbon. As your lunching lady friends sit down with these trays, daintiness is hard to avoid. These are great for keeping your guests moving and mingling.

MATERIALS

2 colors/widths ribbon

Woven bamboo trays

TOOLS

Scissors

● Weave two or more lengths of ribbon through the slats of each tray. Make sure to cut the ribbon long enough to tie knots on both ends.

Off the Rosy Path

This path feels magical, as if it belongs in a fairy tale where only princesses tread. It's perfect for fancy shoes lightly stepping into their ladies' afternoon luncheon.

MATERIALS

16-inch square ceramic tiles

Stix primer (allows paint to adhere to smooth surfaces)

Variety of outdoor floor paint (3 to 5 colors)

Varnish

TOOLS

Paintbrushes or small rollers

Small hand shovel

● Coat the ceramic tiles with primer and go to town with a variety of fun colors.

● To make them last, add a varnish after the paint has dried.

● To make your path feel permanent, trim the grass and level the dirt to settle the tiles into the ground.

Flower Arrangements

Row of Roses

If you're going to throw a pink party, you must visit your local florist, because what shows off pink better than beautiful pink flowers?

MATERIALS

Sheet moss

5 pieces of Oasis floral foam

Greening pins

Flowers, approximately 18

Floral water picks, 2 inches long

● Create a table runner by attaching sheet moss to dry bricks of floral foam with greening pins.

● Your flowers will live for days in your runner if you give them a little water to drink. Just press floral picks into the Oasis every few inches and cut your flower stems to the height of the floral pick. Make it short, make it long—it's completely up to you.

Take-away
Bouquets

Make a beautiful flower arrangement and
a party favor all in one.

···

MATERIALS

A variety of flowers

Covered floral wire

Ribbon, at least 1 inch wide

Fine-point permanent marker

Large basket or bowl

TOOLS

Scissors

Hole punch

Gardening pruners

- For each guest, gather eight or so flowers in your hand, placing the largest bloom in the center and working smaller flowers down and around.

- Wrap a stick of floral wire around the base to hold the arrangement together.

- Tell your guests how you feel about them by attaching a sliver of ribbon labeled with a sweet sentiment that peeks out just above the blooms.

- Place all of the bouquets together in a large basket or bowl.

Pink Petals

What would a garden party be without the help of our friend the flower?

MATERIALS

Cosmos

Snapdragons

Roses

Tulips

Zinnias

Dahlias

When caring for and arranging flowers, here are some helpful hints to keep your blooms fresher longer:

❧ Choose flowers that are almost but not fully mature, as this will ensure a longer cut life.

❧ Hold the stems underwater and cut about 2 inches off, using a sharp knife. Cutting the stems underwater seals the stem with water and prevents air from clogging the stem cells.

❧ Cut stems diagonally to prevent them from resting flat on the bottom of the container.

❧ If floral foam is used, make sure it is saturated with water.

❧ Use a clean vase with fresh warm water.

❧ Mix a floral preservative into the water.

❧ No foliage should be below the waterline in the vase.

❧ Keep flowers away from excessive heat or cold, direct sunlight, or drafts, which will increase transpiration or wilting.

❧ Refresh the water every 2–3 days.

snapdragon

cosmos

rose

tulip

zinnia

dahlia

When I think of people with green thumbs, I tend to think of those rare individuals who can make living things thrive in each of their own special plots.

Herbal
Delight

Sure, people with rambling, formal gardens are to be admired, but I am in awe of the talents of the simpler gardener: the optimistic gardener who can unearth a bit of nature in what appears to be an abandoned lot; the kitchen gardener who harvests ingredients for dinner from a window box; and of course the re-purposer whose imagination can build a garden out of previously used and sometimes mismatched items. It is a core belief of mine that everything old can be new again—that add-ons, adornments, and arrangements can breathe new life into an old concept, and that everyone can find how their hand works best in the garden. I have learned from being an urban apartment dweller as well as a small town citizen that a garden can live where you live, and it can represent who you are, no matter your skill level.

So for this chapter, I channeled the thumbs of all of these fellow gardeners. The lovely fact about herb gardens is that they can live wherever you do. If all you have is a single bucket, no worries—you can still harvest enough basil for tomorrow's pesto sauce. If you have an empty wall against your garage begging to be decorated, you can erect the perfect, eclectic potting shed from an old door and a homemade awning. The best part about being a simple green thumber is that you will not break the bank!

This chapter is all about good solutions for those reluctant to jump into the world of growing. So roll up your sleeves and let's see that green thumb in action!

COOK

NEST

GROW

Virgin Bloody Mary-tini

Spice it up!

SERVES 6-8, DEPENDING ON GLASS SIZE

INGREDIENTS

4 cups chilled tomato or vegetable juice

½ cup fresh lemon juice

½ cup brine from jar of green olives

1½ tablespoons drained bottled horseradish

1 teaspoon Tabasco

½ teaspoon salt

½ teaspoon freshly ground pepper

Celery sticks, gherkins, olives, or lemon slices for garnish

1. Combine all ingredients in a tall pitcher.

2. Pour over ice into tall highball glasses or into chilled martini glasses.

Poached Egg
with Pesto on Puff Pastry Shell

I'm always amazed that the zestiness of pesto is simply a combination of everyday herbs. This is a simple way to make your home cooking look like a gourmet chef's creation.

SERVES 8

INGREDIENTS

1 package puff pastry shells

One 7-ounce jar prepared pesto, at room temperature

2 teaspoons distilled white vinegar

8 fresh eggs

3 medium-size tomatoes, cut into eight ¼-inch slices, at room temperature

Sea salt and freshly ground pepper, to taste

3 tablespoons chopped fresh basil

1. Bake puff pastry shells according to package directions and let cool on a rack. When cool, spread a heaping teaspoon of pesto into the bottom of each shell. Set aside.

2. Fill a deep saucepan with 3 inches of water. Add vinegar and bring to a simmer over medium heat. Crack eggs into the water to poach them until whites are completely cooked and yolks are runny. Remove eggs from the water and dry on paper towels so that the eggs do not make the puff pastry soggy.

3. Place puff pastry shells on 8 salad plates. Place a slice of tomato on each and sprinkle tomato slices with salt, pepper, and fresh basil. Top each with a poached egg and a dollop of pesto.

Fresh Spring Pea Soup
with Herbed Croutons

The subtleness of shallots never ceases to amaze me. And when stirred into this soothing summertime soup, they once again live up to their reputation.

....

SERVES 8

INGREDIENTS

Soup

1 tablespoon olive oil

3 shallots, finely chopped

1 large russet potato, peeled and cubed into ½-inch pieces

4 cups low-sodium chicken broth

4 cups fresh spring peas or frozen baby peas

Salt and white pepper, to taste

¼ cup sour cream (optional)

Croutons

2 tablespoons olive oil

1 tablespoon unsalted butter

1 tablespoon fresh chopped mixed herbs, such as chives, parsley, savory, rosemary, and thyme

3 slices white sandwich bread, crusts removed, cubed into 1-inch pieces

Salt

1. Preheat oven to 325 degrees.

2. In a 4-quart heavy saucepan, heat 1 tablespoon olive oil and sauté the shallots until softened, about 2 minutes.

3. Add potato and cook another 2 minutes, stirring. Add chicken broth and simmer until potato is tender, about 15 minutes.

4. In the meantime, make the croutons. Heat 2 tablespoons olive oil and butter in a large nonstick sauté pan over medium-high heat. When butter is melted, add herbs and sauté until fragrant. Remove from heat and toss with bread cubes. Spread bread cubes in a single layer on a cookie sheet. Season with salt and bake until golden brown, about 15 minutes. Check on croutons every 5 minutes and stir to ensure even browning. Cool croutons on a paper-towel-lined plate. Set aside.

5. Add peas to the broth mixture and simmer until peas are just cooked through, about 2 minutes.

6. Blend with a hand blender right in the pot, or transfer in batches to a blender (be careful when blending hot liquids). Strain soup through a fine-mesh strainer. Place back in pot to reheat. If soup is too thin at this point, you can simmer uncovered to reduce it to the desired consistency. Season with salt and white pepper. Add croutons.

7. Add a dollop of sour cream to the soup along with the herbed croutons.

Orzo Primavera

**A refreshing take on the classic primavera.
Don't forget the basil!**

....

SERVES 8

INGREDIENTS

4 tablespoons olive oil

1 small onion, diced

3 cloves garlic, minced

1 red bell pepper, diced

1 medium green zucchini, diced

1 medium yellow zucchini, diced

½ teaspoon red pepper flakes

3 cups orzo

2 tablespoons lemon juice

Salt and pepper

½ cup chopped basil

½ cup Parmesan cheese

1. Bring a large pot of lightly salted water to a boil over high heat.

2. In the meantime, add 2 tablespoons olive oil and heat in a large sauté pan over medium heat. Add onion, garlic, red pepper, zucchini, and red pepper flakes. Sauté until onions are translucent, about 3 minutes. Place vegetables in a large serving bowl.

3. Add orzo to the boiling water and cook until tender but still firm to the bite. Drain in a colander. Add drained orzo to the vegetables.

4. In a small bowl, whisk together the remaining 2 tablespoons olive oil and lemon juice. Season to taste with salt and pepper. Drizzle vinaigrette over orzo, top with chopped basil and Parmesan cheese, and toss all ingredients to combine. Serve immediately. This can also be made up to 2 hours in advance and served at room temperature.

Cornflake & Fresh
Herb-Crusted Chicken Breasts

Parsley, basil, rosemary. Toss 'em together with your flakes, and you will realize that cornflakes are not just for breakfast anymore.

....

SERVES 6

INGREDIENTS

2 cups crushed cornflakes

4 tablespoons chopped parsley

3 tablespoons chopped basil

2 tablespoons chopped rosemary

2 teaspoons salt

1 teaspoon pepper

6 skinless, boneless chicken breast halves

2 eggs beaten with 1 tablespoon water for egg wash

2 tablespoons vegetable oil

Lemon wedges for garnish

1. Preheat oven to 450 degrees.

2. In a shallow pie pan, combine cornflakes, parsley, basil, rosemary, salt, and pepper.

3. Dip each chicken breast in egg wash and then into corn-flake mixture to coat completely.

4. Coat a cookie sheet with the vegetable oil. Place the coated chicken breasts on the sheet and bake until completely cooked through, 20–25 minutes.

5. Garnish with lemon wedges and serve immediately.

Roasted Fennel
& Carrots with Dill

**Slice it up, chop it up, spice it up, roast it up!
This veggie medley sings the perfect tune.**

....

SERVES 8

INGREDIENTS

**2 fennel bulbs, quartered
and thinly sliced**

**4 large carrots, peeled
and thinly sliced on an angle**

3 tablespoons olive oil

2 tablespoons orange juice

2 tablespoons chopped dill

Salt and pepper

1. Preheat oven to 450 degrees.

2. Toss all ingredients in a large bowl and season with salt and pepper.

3. Spread mixture in a single layer on a shallow pan and cover with foil. Roast for 10 minutes. Remove foil and roast uncovered until vegetables are tender and golden brown, 10 minutes. Serve immediately.

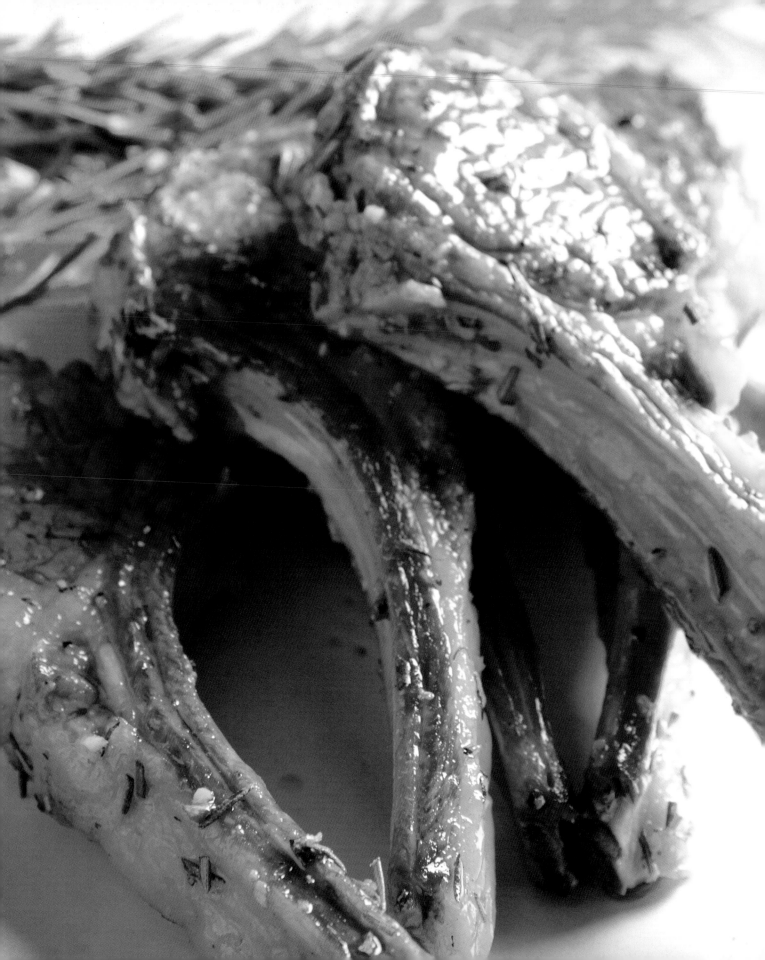

Rosemary & Garlic Lamb Chops
with Mustard Sauce

Easy and elegant, these herbed chops will not disappoint.

SERVES 8

INGREDIENTS

3 tablespoons chopped rosemary

3 tablespoons minced garlic

3 tablespoons olive oil

Eight 1-inch-thick lamb rib chops

1 tablespoon coarse salt

1 tablespoon freshly ground pepper

½ cup white wine

1 cup heavy cream

¼ cup Dijon mustard

Salt and pepper to taste

1. In a shallow baking dish, stir together rosemary, garlic, and 2 tablespoons olive oil. Add lamb chops and turn to coat. Let marinate 20 minutes. Remove chops from marinade and season with salt and pepper.

2. In a large sauté pan, heat remaining 1 tablespoon olive oil until hot but not smoking. Sauté chops in two batches, making sure not to crowd them in the pan. Cook lamb chops approximately 2 minutes per side for medium rare. Transfer to a serving plate and cover with foil to keep warm.

3. In the same sauté pan over medium-high heat, add white wine and deglaze the pan, using a wooden spatula to scrape up all the bits from the bottom of the pan, and simmer until reduced by half. Add heavy cream and simmer until sauce begins to thicken. Whisk in mustard and season with salt and pepper to taste.

4. Pour sauce over lamb chops and serve.

Alfredo Pasta
with Spring Peas & Prosciutto

Peas, parsley, and prosciutto—all three Ps combine for one perfect pasta.

....

SERVES 8

INGREDIENTS

1 pound dried linguini

1 tablespoon olive oil

4 tablespoons butter

½ pound thinly sliced prosciutto, chopped into 1–2-inch pieces

1 medium onion, chopped finely

3 cloves garlic, minced

1 pound fresh peas or one package frozen baby peas

1 jar Alfredo sauce

Salt and pepper

½ cup Parmesan cheese

3 tablespoons chopped parsley

1. In a large pot of salted boiling water, cook linguini until tender but still firm to the bite. Drain pasta and set aside.

2. In a large nonstick sauté pan, heat olive oil with 1 tablespoon butter over medium-high heat. Add prosciutto, onion, and garlic. Cook until onion is translucent, then mix in peas.

3. Heat Alfredo sauce in small saucepan until warmed through.

4. In a large bowl, toss pasta, prosciutto, vegetables, and Alfredo sauce. Season with salt and pepper. Garnish with Parmesan and parsley.

Chunky Tart
Applesauce

If life hands you a bowl of apples, make applesauce . . .

....

SERVES 8

INGREDIENTS

6 pounds Granny Smith apples, peeled, cored, and quartered (12–14 apples)

½ cup packed light brown sugar

1 teaspoon ground cinnamon

1 teaspoon ground nutmeg

¼ teaspoon ground cloves

Pinch of salt

1. Combine all ingredients in a heavy 3-quart saucepan and simmer over low heat until apples are tender and begin to break apart, about 45 minutes. Stir occasionally, but do not overstir, or the apples will break down and the sauce will not be chunky.

2. Serve warm or at room temperature.

Pistachio
Icebox Cookies

...and hopefully it'll hand you cookies to put it on!

MAKES APPROXIMATELY 24 COOKIES

INGREDIENTS

**1 cup unsalted butter,
room temperature**

1 cup light brown sugar

1 egg

1 teaspoon vanilla extract

2 cups all-purpose flour

1 teaspoon baking powder

½ teaspoon salt

**1¼ cups pistachios, shelled
and chopped coarsely**

1. In a medium bowl, cream butter and brown sugar together. Add egg and vanilla and beat until combined.

2. In a separate bowl, whisk together flour, baking powder, and salt. Stir into butter mixture and mix in pistachios.

3. Cover and chill for 1 hour or until dough is firm. Roll chilled dough into 1½–2-inch logs. Wrap logs in wax paper and freeze for 2 hours or overnight.

4. Preheat oven to 400 degrees and grease a cookie sheet.

5. Unwrap dough and cut into ¼-inch slices. Place on prepared cookie sheet and bake until golden brown, 8–10 minutes. Cool slightly on cookie sheets and transfer to racks.

Seating for Three

I love sitting on my patio, just a few yards away from my garden, and this bench is the perfect outdoor creation. It is a great way to turn three dingy chairs into one fantastic bench.

MATERIALS

3 wooden parlor chairs

¾-inch-thick plywood, cut to the width of lined-up chairs

2-inch wood screws

1-inch trim cut to the length of your plywood

Brads

Wood putty

Primer

Exterior paint

TOOLS

Electric drill

Hammer

Paintbrush

- Line up three similar chairs side by side and have a board cut that measures a bit wider and longer than the row of chairs.

- Drill long enough screws through the board and into the chairs.

- Add a decorative trim with small brads, and paint your creation your favorite color.

Copper & Candles

Copper coil, steel wool, and vinegar—doesn't this sound like a kooky science project? Trust me on this one. This project is easy and makes the most elegant candelabra.

MATERIALS

⅝-inch x 10-foot copper coil

Ten 1-inch nails

Ten ½-inch copper bell hangers

10 taper candles

TOOLS

Phillips head screwdriver

PATINA (OPTIONAL)

Vinegar, ½ cup

Salt, 2 teaspoons

Empty squirt bottle

Steel wool

- Stretch and bend a 10-foot copper coil into a spiral about 2½ feet tall. Make sure you round the base out wide enough to keep your creation stable.

- Insert 1-inch nails into the copper bell hangers, and affix them tightly to the copper coil.

- Insert the taper candles and adjust the coil so that the candles stand relatively upright.

- Leave it outdoors and watch as the surface changes. Speed up the patina process by pouring a mixture of ½ cup vinegar with 2 teaspoons of salt into a spray bottle. After distressing the surface with steel wool, coat the copper with this mixture, but make sure to move your candelabra away from any live plants when spraying; this mixture will kill the plants.

A Plant Within a Plant

You water your plants, but have you ever watered your planter? With this project you will: grow your herb garden in a luscious box of organic green moss. When you're finished, this project will look as though it's as much a part of the garden as your plants are.

MATERIALS

Sphagnum moss

Wooden planter

Spray adhesive

Roll of chicken wire

Sheet moss

Floral wire

TOOLS

Staple gun

Wire cutters

Garden gloves

● Affix sphagnum moss to the surface of your entire planter using spray adhesive.

● Staple chicken wire tautly on top of the moss.

● Tie sheet moss on top of the chicken wire with small lengths of floral wire.

● To maintain your moss planter for a longer period of time, fertilize it with fish emulsion weekly.

Out with the Weeds

It can be exhausting work to keep your garden from being overgrown with weeds. You have to carry around your tools, and you end up with piles of weeds in your yard. Well, you don't have to any longer!

MATERIALS

8 screw hooks

Bushel basket

Green acrylic paint

2-inch sticker letters

White rope

TOOLS

Paintbrush

Scissors

● Attach screw hooks around the outside of your bushel basket and hang up your tools. Toss weeds in the basket as you go along.

● Make the basket chic by stenciling on your name using the sticker letters and acrylic paint and adding a braided rope handle.

Green Room

I cannot tell a lie: my thumb is not the greenest thumb around when it comes to planting big, fancy gardens. But small potting projects — now, those I have mastered! This stylish potting area makes my plants (and me) look even better.

....

MATERIALS

3 yards of oilcloth

½-inch grommet kit

5 screw hooks

6-foot wooden pole

Two 3-inch nails

Two 8' x 2" x 2" garden stakes

Table

Shelves

Brackets

Door

TOOLS

Electric Drill

Hammer

• Attach a simple oilcloth awning to the wall with grommets and screw hooks.

• Support the awning by hammering 3-inch nails into the stakes and driving the stakes firmly into the ground, either vertically or diagonally.

• Place your potting table under the awning, and dress up the wall or an old door with mismatched shelves to hold your various tools.

Herbs-a-Plenty

When selecting which herbs to grow, keep in mind the concept of a kitchen garden. Whether you're spicing a salad, baking bread, or creating bath salts, choose the scents and flavors that make you happy.

MATERIALS
Basil
Parsley
Tarragon
Thyme
Rosemary

TIPS

❧ Herbs love sunlight.

❧ Drainage is probably the single most important factor in successful herb growing. Herbs will not grow in wet soil. If you have poor drainage, place a 3-inch layer of crushed stone or similar material on the bottom of the garden.

❧ Avoid adding fertilizer to your soil, as highly fertilized soil tends to create herbs with larger leaves but less flavor.

❧ Fresh leaves may be picked as soon as the plant has enough foliage to maintain growth.

basil

rosemary

thyme

parsley

rosemary

She was born and she
took my breath away.

Here Comes the Sun

She was here and she was beautiful, and she was two months early. Not to worry, though—all fingers, all toes, were accounted for. After a short stay in the hospital, she was actually in our home—in *our* home—hers, mine, and his. Three bugs in a rug. But it was not a well-prepared rug for my new little bug. Due to her early arrival I had only an empty room with a hand-me-down crib that had no sheets. That was it. I started my complicated journey of motherhood a few steps behind.

Next it was bottles, then a high chair. *She is already ready for real lace-up shoes? Two more new teeth? Slow down, you are moving too fast! I have to make your childhood last!* All of a sudden my little girl was days away from her first birthday, and just like her initial descent into this world, this too caught me by surprise. My first child's first birthday party—it is an awesome responsibility and rite of passage for any new mother. I was panicked. But wait a second! I was me . . . a home stylist by trade. If I couldn't throw an all out wing-dinger of a party for my very own child, what good was I? I started where I always start, with color—bright yellow. Next, grown-up fruit salad served in a bowl for the tall people and placed on the end of a stick for the wee ones. Then a smattering of butterflies to make everyone smile, and to engage the older children, we'd plant a garden for them to nurture. Now I was getting somewhere.

I hope this next chapter encourages all mothers to stop and take a breath, so that your child's birthday memories can take flight.

It's all about the kids, but . . . it's so much more fun if you remember the big kids too. So indulge in both of the following creations to create a celebration fit for all ages.

Lillet Fizz

A refreshment for the big kids.

....

SERVES 12

INGREDIENTS

2 bottles (750 ml each) Lillet

3 cups orange juice

½ cup Grand Marnier or other orange-flavored liqueur

1 liter club soda

1 lemon, thinly sliced

1 lime, thinly sliced

1 orange, thinly sliced

1 pint of raspberries

1 bunch of mint

1. Mix ingredients in a large punch bowl and serve over ice.

Lemon-Limeade Sparkler Punch

A refreshment for the little kids.

....

SERVES 12

INGREDIENTS

One 6-ounce can frozen lemonade

One 6-ounce can frozen limeade

1 liter lemon-lime soda

1 lemon, thinly sliced

1 lime, thinly sliced

1 orange, thinly sliced

1. In a large punch bowl, make lemonade and limeade according to package directions.

2. Add soda and fruit and serve.

Grown-up Fruit Salad

Keep the multigenerational vibe going by creating two variations on the basic fruit salad. This one's for the big kids.

SERVES 8

INGREDIENTS

1 cup vanilla yogurt

1 tablespoon confectioners' sugar

¼ cup honey

1 teaspoon vanilla, or ½ vanilla bean, seeds scraped

2 cups cantaloupe, cubed

2 cups honeydew melon, cubed

2 cups seedless red or green grapes, halved

2 kiwis, peeled and sliced

2 cups pineapple chunks

1 cup strawberries, hulled and cut into quarters

Mint leaves for garnish

1. Combine yogurt, confectioners' sugar, honey, and vanilla, and stir. Set aside. (This step can be done in advance and stored in the refrigerator.)

2. Combine fruits in a large bowl and add yogurt dressing. Gently mix to coat all of the fruit.

3. Garnish salad with a sprig of mint leaves and serve immediately.

Fruit Dipsticks

SERVES 8

INGREDIENTS

½ cup vanilla yogurt

One 4-ounce package cream cheese, room temperature

1 tablespoon seedless red raspberry or strawberry jam

1 tablespoon confectioners' sugar

1 teaspoon vanilla

1 cup cantaloupe, cubed or balled

1 cup honeydew melon, cubed or balled

1 cup strawberries, hulled and cut into quarters

Special equipment: 24 flat wooden ice cream spoons

1. Using a hand mixer, beat yogurt, cream cheese, jam, sugar, and vanilla in a large bowl until well combined.

2. Scoop one end of each wooden ice cream spoon into fruit dip until coated. Place on a cookie sheet lined with wax or parchment paper, cover with plastic wrap, and store in the refrigerator. (This step can be done a few hours in advance.)

3. Top each dipstick with one piece of fruit.

Corn Bread
PBJ Triangles

Again, an adult version and a young person's take. Start with a box and end up with a creative creation for young and old. Here's a corn bread kids will love.

SERVES 12–16

INGREDIENTS

2 boxes "Jiffy" Corn Muffin Mix

1 cup smooth peanut butter

1 cup grape jelly

1. Preheat oven to 375 degrees. Grease a 13 x 9 x 2-inch glass baking dish.

2. Prepare corn muffin mix according to package directions. Divide batter in half.

3. Spread half of the batter evenly on the bottom of the baking dish. Top with a layer of peanut butter and dollops of grape jelly. Gently spread the remaining batter on top of the peanut butter and jelly. Cover completely.

4. Bake until corn bread is lightly browned on top and springs back to the touch, 15–20 minutes. Let cool on a baking rack.

Grown-up
Corn Bread Sammies

SERVES 8–10

INGREDIENTS

2 eggs, beaten

1 cup sour cream

2 tablespoons freshly snipped chives

½ tablespoon ground nutmeg

½ cup grated Parmesan cheese

2 boxes "Jiffy" Corn Muffin Mix

½ pound deli ham, thinly sliced

2 Granny Smith apples, peeled, cored, and thinly sliced

½ pound Swiss cheese, thinly sliced

1 lemon

1. Preheat oven to 375 degrees. Grease a 13 x 9 x 2-inch glass baking dish.

2. In a large bowl, combine eggs, sour cream, chives, nutmeg, and Parmesan. Add corn muffin mix and stir gently until just combined (do not overmix).

3. Spread half of the batter on the bottom of the baking dish. Layer ham, apple, and cheese slices on top. Top with the other half of the batter.

4. Bake until top of corn bread is golden brown and springs back to the touch, 15–20 minutes. Let cool on a baking rack.

Spiced Roasted
French Fries

The tall, thin supermodel of every child's culinary delight! What kid doesn't love french fries?

SERVES 8–10

INGREDIENTS

8 russet potatoes, peeled and cut into thick fries

¼ cup olive oil

Salt to taste

2 teaspoons garlic powder

2 teaspoons Italian seasoning

2 teaspoons dried basil

1. Preheat oven to 400 degrees.

2. Toss potatoes and olive oil in a large bowl and season with salt.

3. Combine garlic and herbs in a small bowl and toss with potatoes.

4. Spread potatoes in a single layer on cookie sheets and roast until golden brown and tender, 25–30 minutes.

Puff Pastry au Slaw

A small portion for the little ones, a big flavor for all.

SERVES 8

INGREDIENTS

1 package puff pastry sheets

1 tablespoon fresh lemon juice

¾ cup mayonnaise

½ cup sour cream

1 tablespoon sugar

1 tablespoon poppy seeds

1 package or bunch radishes, thinly sliced

1 package prepared coleslaw vegetable mix containing red and green cabbage and carrots

1 egg

1 tablespoon milk

Special equipment: 2 nonstick muffin tins

1. Thaw puff pastry at room temperature for 30 minutes.

2. Meanwhile make the dressing by combining lemon juice, mayonnaise, sour cream, sugar, and poppy seeds in a small bowl.

3. In a larger bowl, toss radishes and coleslaw mix with dressing. Cover and chill.

4. Preheat oven to 400 degrees. Grease muffin tins. Beat egg with milk for egg wash and set aside.

5. On a lightly floured work surface, unfold a sheet of puff pastry and cut into four equal squares. Repeat with rest of puff pastry.

6. Press pastry squares into prepared muffin tins. Do not allow overlays of puff pastry to touch. Brush lightly with egg wash.

7. Bake until golden brown, 10–15 minutes. Allow to cool in muffin tins and gently remove when cooled.

8. Fill nests with slaw just before serving.

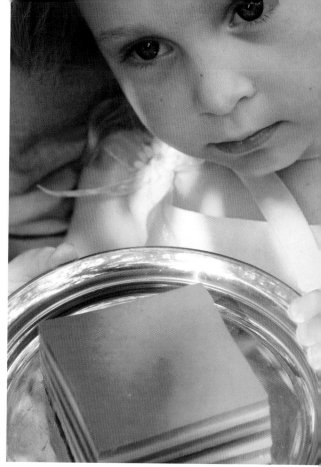

Rainbow Jell-O

It wasn't a party at my house unless my mother prepared the rainbow Jell-O. Slowly, meticulously, she would put together her own layered pot of gold before every celebration.

SERVES 15–18

INGREDIENTS

5 small packages Jell-O in different flavors and colors (red, green, yellow, blue, orange)

One 16-ounce container sour cream

1. Working with one flavor at a time, make one recipe of Jell-O by following directions on box and divide in half (½ cup each).

2. Add 3 tablespoons water to one half and pour into an 8 x 10-inch glass baking dish. Place in the refrigerator and chill until firm.

3. Add ⅓ cup sour cream to remaining half, set aside at room temperature, and then pour on top of the previously chilled layer.

4. Chill again and repeat the process with remaining Jell-O packages. The 5 packages will yield 10 layers.

Butterfly
Ice Cream Sandwiches

You blink, and a butterfly is gone.
It's the same with these ice cream sandwiches!

....

SERVES 10

INGREDIENTS

1 package sugar cookie dough, well chilled

1 pint chocolate ice cream, slightly softened

1 pint raspberry or mixed berry sorbet, slightly softened

1 pint mango or passion fruit sorbet, slightly softened

Special equipment: Butterfly-shaped cookie cutter

1. Preheat oven to 350 degrees.

2. On a lightly floured work surface, roll out dough to ⅛ inch thickness, using additional flour as needed to prevent sticking. Cut out butterfly shapes and gently brush off any excess flour. Transfer butterfly shapes to ungreased cookie sheets and bake until lightly golden brown, 8–10 minutes. Remove from cookie sheets and place on racks to cool.

3. Top half of the butterflies with the different ice creams and sorbets and then place another cookie on top of the ice cream. Press gently.

4. Cover and freeze the sandwiches. Arrange in a chilled glass bowl to serve. These can be made 4 days ahead.

Lollipop Cupcake
Garden

Willy Wonka's got nothing on these dressed-up store-bought delicacies.

....

SERVES 24

INGREDIENTS

1 box yellow or chocolate cake mix

1 container chocolate frosting

1 package Oreos, crushed

24 lollipops

Mint leaves for leaf garnish

1. Following directions on the cake mix box, make cupcakes. Let cool on a baking rack.

2. Frost cupcakes and coat with crushed Oreos.

3. Place a lollipop in the middle of the cupcake and garnish the "root" of the lollipop with one mint leaf.

Create-a-Plate

You only need to know a few simple geometric shapes to make this most useful table mat. Just set your places with contact paper.

MATERIALS

Vinyl, cut to fit your tabletop

4 colors of contact paper, 3 yards of each

1 piece of card stock

TOOLS

Scissors

Dinner plate

Straight edge

Measuring tape

● Circles make for an easy plate (or trace a real dinner plate).

● To make the cutlery, just use your grade-school geometry—an oval for the bowl of a spoon, a rectangle for the tines of a fork, and a triangle for the knife blade. Make it easy by creating templates so you only have to measure once.

● To store your table mat for future use, hang it over a closet rod or on a clip hanger. Folding or rolling your mat will create creases in the contact paper.

Hoop Hoop Hooray!

I've always loved a good hula hoop. I used to keep mine going for so long my stomach would hurt. Instead of hooping it up, we're *hanging* it up and topping off this sunny party with fabulous, fluttery fringe.

....

MATERIALS

3 bright solid fabrics, 3 yards

1 bright patterned fabric, 3 yards

3 hula hoops

10 artificial butterflies, wired

TOOLS
Pinking shears

- Using pinking shears, cut various scraps of brightly colored fabric into different lengths and different widths and knot them onto hula hoops.

- Make it feel even more flighty by twisting wired butterflies onto the ends of some pieces of fabric.

- Use strips of scrap fabric to make a hanger.

Sweet Wings

When my daughter crawled around the house on her first birthday wearing these wings, the entire room took notice. You'll have many happy children and many entertained adults with these sweet wings.

MATERIALS

2 wire hangers

White fishnet stockings

2 wooden drawer pulls

Bright-colored paints

Craft glue

2 pieces of ¾-inch elastic cut in 16-inch pieces

Pipe cleaners

TOOLS

Wire cutters

● Cut the wire hooks off both wire hangers and twist each hanger into a figure 8 shape, with the point of the hanger in the center of the 8.

● Insert the first figure 8 hanger into the fishnet stockings, one wing per leg. Insert the second hanger into the bunched-up remainder of the stockings, stretching the fishnets tautly around the hangers. Make sure to line up the two points of the hangers.

● Fasten the pipe cleaner around the waistline of the stockings and around the points of the wire hangers.

● To make the arm straps, tie a knot to create a circle in each separate piece of elastic. Secure the circles to the back of the wings by wrapping another pipe cleaner through the elastic loops and around the center of the wings.

● Paint the wooden drawer pulls in bright colors. Let dry.

● Attach the wooden drawer pulls over the sharp pointed parts of the hangers with craft glue.

Googly Eyes
& Smiles

Fill these bags, and then fill the hands of your little party guests with festive and fun favors.

MATERIALS

Pipe cleaners

Paper gift bags

Googly eyes

TOOLS

Craft glue

● Punch pipe cleaners into the sides of regular-size gift bags, bend them into the shape of butterfly wings, and glue the ends to the inside of the bags.

● Give the kids a giggle by adding googly eyes on the bags and attaching a brown pipe cleaner to the bag handles as antennae.

Backyard Butterflies

There is a world of benefit to children learning their way around the garden. At this backyard butterfly bonanza, give your little guests a row to call their own and a sweet butterfly with which to mark it.

MATERIALS

Metal garden stakes

Rubberize-It, 2 colors

Floral wire

TOOLS

Gloves

Wire cutters

Sharpie pen

• Wearing gloves, dip a metal garden stake into Rubberize-It liquid plastic to make the body. (Note: Periodically seal the can of Rubberize-It and shake it to prevent the product from drying out).

• Make the wings by slowly dipping teardrop-shaped wire pieces into a different color of Rubberize-It.

• Let the wings and body dry separately before putting them together. An easy way to dry your butterfly wings and garden stakes is to stick them into a pot of sand.

• Write the name of the plant on the center stake before attaching the wings.

• *Never* let children use Rubberize-It without adult supervision!

Beanstalks & Beyond

I can't wait to show my little daughter how a garden grows. I feel the best way to introduce her to it is by choosing quick-growing, big-blossoming plants.

FAST-GROWING PLANTS

String beans

Butter lettuce

Sugar snap peas

Radishes

Sunflowers

Poppies

❧ Using standard potting soil, dig multiple rows of troughs, and plant seeds in a random pattern, placing taller plants such as sunflowers in the back. Cover the seeds with dirt, and gently pat them with your hand. Water twice per day until the seeds germinate. Water gently so as not to disturb the seeds. After they begin to sprout, water once a day or every other day. Once the seeds sprout, measure about 8 inches from one plant to another, removing the plants in between.

❧ Plant a children's garden that will grow quickly—kids love immediate gratification. These plants germinate in 5–14 days. (You can even plant seedlings for faster results.)

❧ String beans and snow peas are fun because your kids can eat them right off the plant.

❧ Vegetables with large seeds will sprout faster.

❧ Have your child start a garden journal. Have him or her measure, water, and observe the changes to the garden daily.

❧ Kids like extremes. Play with bright colors and large flowers such as sunflowers.

❧ Keep plants pesticide-free for the safety of your child.

I must admit that at the
conclusion of a busy summer,
I welcome the signs of fall.

Rustic
Woods

Perhaps it is because warm weather gathers friends, family, and neighbors like moths to a flame. In my family we have always celebrated the long days and bright sunshine with open arms and infinite invitations. Just when I think I cannot attend one more fun-filled, sunshine-drenched, crowded party, the season that offers a little peace and quiet arrives, when the days grow shorter and the nights grow longer. Not a moment too soon, the roar of the sea is replaced with the rustling of leaves, and my desire to party is replaced with the thought of curling up in the warmth of a loved one.

I always think of autumn as such an intimate time of year; a soothing time, from the comfort food we prepare to the thick and protective clothes we wrap around our bodies. Fall is the time of year for cuddling—not cold enough to be completely protected from the harsh weather but brisk enough to pull others close. You may find yourself fireside with a sweetheart, warming your hands on a mug of toasty soup with a small group of friends. Or perhaps you are exploring the woods with your child, gathering branches, twigs, and stones from Mother Nature's floor to add décor in and around your home. I love the special silence about the fall. The hum that only fall possesses.

I hope this chapter encourages you to revel in the quiet and notice the delicate and subtle changes that a new season brings. Create a rustic, romantic setting outside your home using nature's textural objects. Prepare a feast with root veggies and seasoned nuts that accompany this time of year so well. Embrace the fall—and while you are at it, embrace the loved one sitting next to you.

Mulled Cranberry
Apple Cider

My mother made the yummiest hot mulled cider. It would fill our house with great smells and much love. Here's my take on my mother's warming brew.

SERVES 12

INGREDIENTS

7 cups apple cider

5 cups cranberry juice

2 oranges, zested and juiced

1 bay leaf

3 cinnamon sticks

4 whole cloves

1 lemon, sliced

1 tablespoon packed brown sugar

1 inch peeled ginger root, sliced

Pinch of salt

1½ cups brandy

½ cup Triple Sec, or other orange-flavored liqueur

1. Combine all ingredients except brandy and Triple Sec in a large saucepan. Bring to a boil, then lower the heat to a simmer for 20 minutes.

2. Turn heat to low just to keep the cider warm. Before serving, add the brandy and the Triple Sec, and strain into mugs.

Roasted & Spiced
Mixed Nuts

This little outdoor treat is a bit more effort than a trail mix but well worth it when enjoying the great outdoors.

SERVES 8

INGREDIENTS

1 cup almonds

1 cup peanuts

1 cup cashews

½ cup pumpkin seeds

¼ cup sunflower seeds

2 tablespoons olive oil

2 tablespoons butter, melted

½ teaspoon salt

1 teaspoon cayenne pepper

1 teaspoon garlic powder

1. Preheat oven to 300 degrees.

2. Combine all nuts and seeds in a large bowl. Toss with olive oil and melted butter, salt, cayenne pepper, and garlic powder.

3. Spread seasoned mixture on a cookie sheet and roast for 20–25 minutes, stirring frequently.

4. Remove from oven. Spread mixture on a rack to cool, and serve.

Pureed
Squash Soup

What better way to warm yourself and fill your belly than with a mug full of soup made from the harvest of the season? Go ahead — wrap your hands around this autumn beauty.

SERVES 8

INGREDIENTS

4 tablespoons butter

3 cloves garlic, chopped

1 medium onion, chopped

1 tablespoon chopped thyme

1 russet potato, peeled and cut into 1-inch cubes

Two 14½-ounce cans low-sodium chicken stock

Two 12-ounce packages frozen winter squash, thawed

1 cup heavy cream

½ teaspoon nutmeg

Salt

1. Melt 4 tablespoons butter in a large pot over medium heat. Add garlic, onion, and thyme and cook until onion is translucent, 3–4 minutes.

2. Add potato and chicken stock and bring to a simmer. Continue simmering until potato is cooked through.

3. Add winter squash and cook until heated through.

4. Transfer soup in batches to a blender and puree until smooth. Add back to the pot and bring to a simmer to heat through. Add heavy cream and nutmeg and season with salt to taste.

Chicken Pot Pie

A chicken pot pie can really warm the soul. It may seem intimidating, but by combining these prepackaged ingredients, you'll find it doesn't have to be hard.

....

SERVES 8

INGREDIENTS

2 tablespoons olive oil

2 cloves garlic, chopped

1 medium onion, chopped

2 ribs celery, chopped

1 tablespoon chopped thyme, or ½ tablespoon dried thyme

2 pounds boneless, skinless chicken breasts, cut into 1-inch chunks

2 cans prepared chicken or turkey gravy

2 russet potatoes, peeled and cut into ½-inch cubes

½ cup heavy cream

One 16-ounce bag frozen mixed vegetables

Salt and pepper to taste

1 box frozen puff pastry sheets, thawed

1. Preheat oven to 400 degrees.

2. Heat olive oil over medium heat in a large saucepan. Add garlic, onion, celery, and thyme and cook until onion is translucent, 3–4 minutes.

3. Add chicken pieces in batches and brown chicken on all sides. Do not crowd the chicken or it will not brown. Remove chicken from pan and set aside.

4. Add gravy and potato and simmer until potato is just cooked through.

5. Add heavy cream to gravy and vegetable mixture and stir. Add chicken and frozen vegetables and stir to combine. Season with salt and pepper and remove from heat.

6. Unroll one puff pastry sheet.

7. Pour chicken mixture into a 10-inch iron skillet or casserole dish. Top with puff pastry sheet and bake at 400 degrees for 25–30 minutes, until puff pastry is puffed and golden. Serve immediately.

Beefy Stew

A hearty stew is never wrong when served against the rustic backdrop of autumn. A cold winter is approaching, so don't be afraid to put some meat on your bones.

....

SERVES 8

INGREDIENTS

2 tablespoons olive oil

2 pounds beef stew meat

½ cup flour

4 russet potatoes, peeled and cut into 1-inch cubes

1 small package baby carrots

1 package pearl onions, peeled

1 package button mushrooms, cut into quarters

8 cloves garlic, peeled

2 cans Guinness beer

2 cans beef broth

4 sprigs thyme

4 sprigs rosemary

Salt and pepper

1. Preheat oven to 350 degrees.

2. In a large stockpot, heat olive oil over medium-high heat. Dredge stew meat in flour and drop into pan in batches. Cook until nicely browned on all sides. Set aside until all the meat is browned.

3. Add potatoes, carrots, pearl onions, button mushrooms, and garlic. Cook 2 minutes. Return meat to pan.

4. Pour in beer and broth. Add sprigs of thyme and rosemary. Cover, and simmer on medium-low heat 45–60 minutes, until meat and vegetables are tender. Season with salt and pepper to taste.

Beef Pasties

In the early industrial days of Michigan, coal miners used to fill their pockets with freshly baked pasties. Not only did these lunchtime treats provide a hearty meal, but they also served as warming pockets for those bitterly cold, hard workdays. This tradition is kept alive in my home state by roadside stands where every hand-painted sign claims to serve the best pasty ever.

SERVES 4

INGREDIENTS

1 pound ground beef

1 onion, finely chopped

1 russet potato, finely chopped

Salt and pepper to taste

2 boxes ready-made pie crust

1 egg, beaten

1. Preheat oven to 425 degrees.

2. In a medium-size bowl, mix ground beef, onion, potato, salt, and pepper.

3. Cut pie crust rounds in half.

4. On one side of each half, place a small handful of mixture, and fold the other side of the dough over the meat, creating a triangle shape.

5. Gently press along the edges to seal the pasty, and brush with beaten egg. Place on cookie sheet.

6. Bake at 425 degrees for 15 minutes, then lower to 325 degrees and bake until crust is golden brown, an additional 45 minutes.

Spinach Salad

This salad mirrors the ruggedness of the great outdoors with its deep greens, crisp bacon, and pungent cheese.

....

SERVES 8

INGREDIENTS

12 slices bacon

1 tablespoon olive oil

2 shallots, finely chopped

3 tablespoons sherry vinegar

½ teaspoon salt

1 teaspoon pepper

2 cups whole grain croutons

Three 10-ounce packages ready-to-use baby spinach

1 small red onion, cut into thin rings

2 cups crumbled blue cheese

1. In a saucepan, cook bacon over low heat to render fat. Cook until bacon is crispy. Remove bacon from pan, and drain on paper towels. When cool, chop bacon coarsely.

2. To the pan with the bacon drippings, add olive oil and shallots. Cook shallots over medium heat until translucent, 3–4 minutes. Remove from heat and whisk in vinegar, salt, and pepper. Add croutons and stir to combine. Cover to keep warm.

3. Place spinach in a large bowl. Top with red onion and blue cheese. Drizzle dressed croutons and vinaigrette over the top and serve immediately.

Brussels Sprouts
& Onion Hobo Packs

Try 'em, you might love 'em.

SERVES 8

INGREDIENTS

2 pounds baby brussels sprouts

8 tablespoons olive oil

3 tablespoons chopped thyme

Salt and pepper

One 12-ounce jar roasted red peppers, drained and chopped

1 garlic clove, finely chopped

¼ cup grated Parmesan cheese

4 large onions, sliced into sixteen ½-inch slices

1. Preheat grill to medium-high heat, or preheat oven to 400 degrees.

2. In a small bowl, combine brussels sprouts, 4 tablespoons olive oil, 2 tablespoons thyme, and salt and pepper to taste.

3. In another small bowl, combine red peppers, garlic, Parmesan, 1 tablespoon olive oil, 1 tablespoon thyme, and salt and pepper to taste.

4. Lay out 16 squares of aluminum foil.

5. Divide brussels sprouts among 8 sheets.

6. Lay two onion slices on each of the other 8 sheets, drizzle with remaining olive oil, and top with red pepper mixture.

7. Roll edges of foil together, and seal into packets.

8. Cook on grill for 20–25 minutes or bake for 25 minutes.

Nutty Caramel
Apples

Who says making caramel apples has to be difficult?

．．

SERVES 8

INGREDIENTS

One 14-ounce bag caramels, unwrapped

8 small apples

1 cup mixed salted nuts, finely chopped

SPECIAL EQUIPMENT

Popsicle sticks, cut down to 5-inch lengths

1. Place caramels in a saucepan and melt over low heat.

2. Insert Popsicle sticks in apples and dip apples in caramel. Allow excess to drip.

3. Roll caramel-covered apples in nuts.

4. Place on wax paper–lined cookie sheets to set.

5. Refrigerate, or serve when cool.

While You Were Out

There are so many activities to do outdoors, and when I was growing up in a large family before the age of cell phones, it was hard to keep track of everybody's whereabouts. Sure, you can cover your countertop with reminder Post-its—or you can create this great-looking, rustic outdoor message board.

MATERIALS

Wood panel

Magnetic paint

Red exterior paint

Painter's tape

Halved wood logs (approximately 6)

Long screws

Strong magnets

Several 1-inch pieces of twig

Stones

Short screws

Picture wire

TOOLS

Foam brush

Drill

Glue gun

Screwdriver

Garden pruners

● Cover a piece of wood in magnetic paint, let dry, and then paint over it with a bright color.

● Using your drill and long screws, attach the halved logs around the border of your sign.

● Magnets can be adorned with anything found on Mother Nature's floor. We chose stones and hot-glued them onto strong magnets, but you can use small pinecones, sticks, or acorns.

● Make the board personal by writing your family name out of twigs.

● Attach a picture wire on the back for the option to hang your sign.

Seat Warmers

In the cool fall weather, you want warmth all around you—on your head, around your neck, and why not on your seat? With a minimal amount of fabric and a lack of sewing ability, you can simply dust off your worn-out chairs and give them their own snuggly shawl for the upcoming cold weather.

MATERIALS

Director's-style chair

1 yard fleece fabric

TOOLS

Measuring tape

Pinking shears

Straight pins

● Measure the back and seat of the chair.

● For the back, add 4 inches to the width and double the height. Cut a piece of fabric to this size with pinking shears.

● Fold the fabric over the chair back and pin in place. Make sure it is centered, which means you have 2 inches of extra fabric on either side.

● Measure 1 inch down from the top of the chair back, and cut a 2-inch-long strip in the extra fabric on each side of chair, front and back. Knot these ties together securely. Repeat, starting at the bottom of the chair back. Knot the ties securely.

● Trim off the remaining extra fabric.

● Measure the seat length (the distance from front to back), then double it and add 12 inches to determine the length of the fabric to cut. For the width, just add one inch to the measurement of the width of the seat. Cut the fabric to these measurements.

● Fold the seat fabric in half lengthwise and pin together.

● Cut out 2 square shapes from the pinned side of the fabric, leaving a 2-inch strip on either end and one down the center (it will look like an uppercase E).

● Unpin the seat fabric, center over the seat of your chair, and tie 3 strips underneath to secure.

A Table
from the Trees

Walking through the woods behind my cottage on Lake Michigan, I've always dreamed of ways to turn fallen branches and tree trunks into something useful. This is a project that is born from Mother Earth and can live in her outdoors with perfect harmony. With just a stroll through your backyard (and a stroll through your craft store), you can gather all the materials you need for your table.

MATERIALS

Leaves for tracing (real or artificial)

12 Basswood Country Rounds (available at your local craft store)

Walnut stain

36 x 36-inch plywood, ¾ inch thick

Wood glue

Exterior varnish

3 chunky logs, about 24 inches high

TOOLS

Pencil

Craft wood-burner tool

Sponge or rag

Paintbrush

- Use your pencil to trace various leaf shapes onto wooden rounds.

- Slowly follow pencil lines using a medium tip on your wood-burning tool. If you move the tool too quickly, the wood does not have time to burn. Keep the burning tool moving as you see the line becoming a dark burned tone. Repeat for all 12 rounds.

- Use the sponge or rag to apply stain to the plywood. Allow time for it to dry completely.

- Arrange the rounds around the outside of the plywood, and use wood glue to secure. Let dry for 24 hours.

- Varnish the entire tabletop, starting with the rounds and working your way to the middle.

- Complete at least two coats according to the directions of your particular varnish.

- When the tabletop is completely dry, arrange the three logs in a triangle and place the tabletop on them. We left the tabletop and base unattached for easier placement and storage. If you prefer, you can drill and screw the top to the base.

A Flicker
in the Woods

Make your candles feel at home in the forest by giving them a little lift. During an evening in the great outdoors, nothing sets a more natural mood than the light of a candle.

....

MATERIALS

Pillar candle

Eight to ten 6-inch twigs

6 pieces of 6-inch twig garland

TOOLS

Gardening pruners

Awl

Glue gun

- Dig out the base of the candle and hot-glue a bundle of similar-size sticks and twigs to the base.

- Trim the sticks to an even length, and you've made nature's own candlestick.

A Timber Trail

"Stopping by woods on a snowy evening" and "Over the river and through the woods"—these phrases come to mind as I tiptoe on this organic path, made from cedar posts and mulch.

MATERIALS

8-foot cedar posts (one per path step)

6-inch ground staples (4 per path step)

Mulch

TOOLS

Measuring tape

Chain saw

● Cut the cedar posts and lay them down in multiple rectangular shapes.

● To keep the posts grounded, secure them with ground staples.

● Fill the open rectangles with mulch.

Much Mulch

Most people think of mulch as a necessity, but honestly, I think of it as a decorative element—an accessory, if you will. The necklace to the tree, the bracelet to the bush. So, just as you wouldn't put on your little black dress without your high heels, don't forget to accessorize your landscaping.

TIPS

Mulch helps control weeds by blocking out sunlight needed for their growth.

Natural mulch adds organic matter to the soil, which enhances the quality of the garden.

If you choose to add a barrier under the mulch, try newspaper. It's biodegradable and won't permanently alter the state of your garden.

Mulch encourages earthworms, which aerate the soil.

You'll need approximately 1 cubic yard of mulch for every 100 square feet of area to be covered.

cedar

pine bark

mini chips

red cedar

soil conditioner

black cedar

Picture
Index

COOK

Main Dishes on the Grill

Beer-simmered
Grilled Brats, 19
Backyard Reunion

Cheese-stuffed
Turkey Burgers, 19
Backyard Reunion

BBQ Chicken Drumsticks, 20
Backyard Reunion

Grilled Red Snapper
with Ginger Marinade, 48
Down by the Sea

Grilled Jerk Shrimp Skewers
with Watermelon Salsa, 51
Down by the Sea

My Mom's Planked
Whitefish, 53
Down by the Sea

Main Dish

"Not-So-Tea" Sandwiches, 80
Garden Party

Spicy Turkey Sausage Skewers
over Tossed Arugula, 85
Garden Party

Cornflake & Fresh Herb-
Crusted Chicken Breasts, 107
Herbal Delight

Rosemary & Garlic Lamb Chops
with Mustard Sauce, 111
Herbal Delight

Alfredo Pasta with Spring
Peas & Prosciutto, 113
Herbal Delight

Corn Bread PBJ Triangles, 133
Here Comes the Sun

Grown-up Corn Bread
Sammies, 133
Here Comes the Sun

Chicken Pot Pie, 165
Rustic Woods

Beefy Stew, 166
Rustic Woods

Beef Pasties, 168
Rustic Woods

COOK

PROJECTS

Desserts

Mixed Berry &
Pound Cake Trifle, 24
Backyard Reunion

Chilled Watermelon Slices
with Lime, Juice, Honey
& Mint, 25
Backyard Reunion

Billy Goat Cookies, 27
Backyard Reunion

Easy Vanilla Bean Flan, 57
Down by the Sea

Layered Ice Cream Cake, 87
Garden Party

Chunky Tart Applesauce, 114
Herbal Delight

Pistachio Icebox Cookies, 115
Herbal Delight

Fruit Dipsticks, 130
Here Comes the Sun

Rainbow Jell-O, 139
Here Comes the Sun

Butterfly Ice Cream
Sandwiches, 141
Here Comes the Sun

Lollipop Cupcake Garden, 142
Here Comes the Sun

Nutty Caramel Apples, 173
Rustic Woods

Tabletop

Painted Tabletop, 28
Backyard Reunion

Food Covers, 29
Backyard Reunion

BBQ Baskets, 31
Backyard Reunion

Brown Bag Burgers, 31
Backyard Reunion

Pails of Pop, 32
Backyard Reunion

In the Lap of Luxury, 88
Garden Party

Create-a-Plate, 144
Here Comes the Sun

PROJECTS

Outdoor Furniture

Outdoor Décor

Lighting

Party Invitations and Giveaways

GARDEN

Path

Off the Rosy Path, 90
Garden Party

A Timber Trail, 182
Rustic Woods

Garden

Gardens-a-Plenty, 37
Backyard Reunion

Floating Flora, 69
Down by the Sea

Pink Petals, 96
Garden Party

Out with the Weeds, 119
Herbal Delight

Green Room, 120
Herbal Delightt

Herbs-a-Plenty, 122
Herbal Delight

Backyard Butterflies, 152
Here Comes the Sun

Beanstalks & Beyond, 154
Here Comes the Sun

Much Mulch, 182
Rustic Woods

Fountain

Sounds of the Sea, 67
Down by the Sea

Floral

Row of Roses, 93
Garden Party

Takeaway Bouquets, 95
Garden Party

Planter

Tin Planters, 35
Backyard Reunion

A Plant Within a Pant, 119
Herbal Delight

ACKNOWLEDGMENTS

I often think it is not right that my name appears in big bold script on the cover of my books when it was truly a dedicated group that brought these pages to life. A group who sacrificed, fought, and pushed in the hopes that their work might inspire an individual to make a young child's party more festive, a family celebration more meaningful, and a backyard more inviting. A group who tried again and again to perfect a recipe or make a project simpler so that readers might enjoy the art of outdoor living to its fullest.

To the group of talented individuals who sweated, laughed, stubbed their toes, and swore they could work no harder (and then did anyway) during the development and production of this book:

Amanda Kingloff. When I feel I cannot push any harder, I watch you battle onward with quiet grace and dedication. You continue to rise to any occasion that comes our way with great elegance. All of this inspires me daily. Yes, you guessed it, when I grow up, I hope to be just like you!

Stephanie Di Tullio. Thank you for having faith enough to travel far in order to be a part of this and for taking our projects to a whole new level of sophistication. And thank you, of course, for the Diana Mason-like references that made me smile in even the darkest hours.

Gretchen Hauge. I am so glad you agreed to throw your car keys in the hedges and join in. I am still not sure we were worthy of your collection of vintage clothes and Wisconsin-inspired dishes.

Leah Hays. Watching you lean in — then jump in — has been one of the best experiences of my career. Your culinary flower is just beginning to blossom, and I can't wait to sit back and watch.

Pam Healey and the entire crew at Lynch's Garden Center in Southampton. You will never know how your contributions helped fill our pages and push this little engine that could way higher than it would otherwise have gone.

Brian Maynard and the whole KitchenAid team. Your continued faith and support for your home-state girl heats our food, refrigerates our flowers, and mixes our dough. Thank you.

Tommy Paulk, Dennis Thomas, and the whole team at Bonnie Plants. Thank you for putting your faith behind my brand and for your devoted support of our production.

Paul Whicheloe. When I turned to you in the wee hours of the morning to start all over again, you supported my vision and did not throw in the towel. It was a moment I will never forget and for which I will be forever grateful.

Evan McGann. Your attitude is one in a million. Your quiet humor and gentle grumblings make me and all the others smile.

Brice Gaillard, the Southern belle of the bunch. Oh how I love when you are near! Your funny take on the world is such a pleasure, not to mention your styling eye and expert little touches that never leave us.

Jackie Lowey and Rebecca and Jonathan Kuperschmid; India Galesi Grant and Christina Galesi; Lisa, David, Adelia, and Evvie Rattray; Mary Grace and Joanne Patrick; Rianna, Brandon, and Jamie Helier; Erica Payne; Susan Early-Helman and Edwina, Katie, and Dorothy Annicelli, who dressed up and showed up to be a part of this publication. Your images are like candy on my pages — thank you for your bright eyes and bold smiles.

Ira Silverberg. Boy oh boy, do you have a steady, constant hand that I always feel is resting right on the small of my back for whenever I need a bit of support and guidance.

Jill Cohen. You are sorely missed. Your passion is unmatchable and your dedicated eye and thoughts were such a part of this book, making our content all it could be.

Gary Tooth. Will I ever be worthy of your design? The ease with which you seem to place images on a page gives this book much of its style. Thank you.

Nancy Banks, Sarah Essex, Tori Horowitz, Mariska Hargitay, and Martha McCully. Thank you for understanding the long periods of silence from your workaholic friend. I adore and cherish you all.

Mom, Dad, Lynn, Marlee, Bing, Dan, Bob, Meredith, Paul, Charlie, Jack, Mimi, Tilly, Quattro, and Maverick. The memories that you have provided me with fill these pages. I wonder why fate's fortune shined on me, thus enabling me to call you all family.

My new family — Patsy, Jimmy, Dick, Gail, Bridgit, Bud, Sandra, Corey, Isaac, Corbin, John, Lillian. You must often ask, where has our newest family member gone? Yet you seem to hold no grudges when I reappear after creating a book like this. Thank you for not judging my overworked self. And beware — your stories will soon appear in pages just like these.

And finally to the girl who brightens up every moment of my day — my little one, Prentiss Crockett Corbin. How lucky I am to call you my daughter.